EMINENT DOGS
DANGEROUS MEN

Donald McCaig

The Lyons Press

Printed in the United States of America

10 9 8 7 6 5 4 3 2

Library of Congress Cataloging-in-Publication Data
McCaig, Donald.
    Eminent dogs, dangerous men / Donald McCaig.
        p.   cm.
    Originally published: 1st ed. New York, NY : E. Burlingame
Books, c1991.
    ISBN 1-55821-670-7 (pbk.)
    1. Border collie—Anecdotes. 2. Sheep dogs—Scotland—
Anecdotes. 3. Sheep   dog   trials—Scotland—Anecdotes.
4. McCaig, Donald—Journeys—Scotland. 5. Novelists, Ameri-
can—20th century—Biography. 6. Sheep ranchers—Virginia—
Biography. 7. Scotland—Description and travel. I. Title.
[SF429.B64M38   1998]
636.737'4—dc21   98-14735
                                                           CIP

EMINENT DOGS
DANGEROUS MEN

For Anne—
who kept the home fires burning

Of course you should talk to your dogs.
But talk sense!

J. M. WILSON

1

Running with the Big Hats

I saved his life once. It's wild down by our river, shaded by shale cliffs that contain the river's wanderings. Old-timers talk of skating parties on the ice: hissing blades, kids' yells, a bonfire crackling on the pebbly bank; but the river has only frozen hard once in the twenty years we've lived on the farm.

It was late January, a still morning, brutally cold. Winter hung from every tree, and the glaze on the alder stems poking through the river ice—that glaze was winter, too. The dog's toenails clicked on the ice. Pip's tail was a gallant plume as he skated toward the far shore and in.

He's a strong swimmer. During the dog days of July, he spends hours down here paddling around. Quick as he was in, he turned and tried to haul himself back onto the ice. He scratched at the slickness and paddled so hard his chest came clear of the water, but he found no purchase. The current sucked at his hindquarters, and he fell back. Again and again. When he tired, the river would take him under the ice downstream until he lodged somewhere.

Since the water came only to my rib cage, it wasn't particularly brave going in after him, but, my, it was brisk. I hurled Pip onto the ice and addressed the matter of my own return to dry land, which was rather more difficult than I had imagined. When Pip ran back to help, I shouted him away. It's true what they say: If you flatten out on the ice, it bears more weight, and that's how I scootched to shore.

As I hurried up the lane to the house, my pants legs stiffened and gleamed. Pip circled me—ice in his belly hair, ice in his ruff—something like wonder in his wide eyes. He is a four-year-old, forty-pound, black-and-white dog. I am a forty-five-year-old human. Sometimes the souls of unalike species can marry.

He's the first working dog I've ever owned. He sleeps beside my bed at night. After we've spent a day wrestling sheep through manure-filthy pens, I stand him in a shower before I let him into the rest of the house.

Since Pip was two, we've been running in sheepdog trials. Sometimes we've done well, usually not. We've run in the novice classes with other inexperienced handlers and their inexperienced dogs. We've never run against the Big Hats.

Pip's life hasn't always been happy. When we had foot rot in the flock, he worked every single day while my wife trimmed feet. It was hot and it was angry and bloody and covered with blood and pus and flies. At the end of the day my wife would be in tears, and the exhausted dog would drag himself into the corner, too tired to eat his dinner. I've used him on cows with young calves and winced as he dodged their charge, their hoofs. I've worked him too long and too hard in the sun. Few marriages are uninterrupted bliss.

Pip has aspirations. In the next turn of the karmic wheel, he hopes to return as a flamenco dancer: starched white shirt, black pants, proud castanets.

Like some princes, he frets about poison and suspiciously sniffs each scrap offered from your fingers though it's identical to the scrap of a moment ago.

His nickname is Broadway Joe.

He knows that men only kick the contemptible, and he won't be touched—even gently—by human feet.

Pip's what sheepdog men call "hyper." He's too rapid, rather too keen, and that can get him into trouble. Livestock appreciate a calm, deliberate dog and will accord it respect. A jumpy, down-again, up-again dog makes them skittish.

A Border Collie moves livestock by controlled intimidation. He pushes them along with a threatening glare. This glare is called "eye" and is probably related to the wolves' tactic of selecting a victim in a herd by catching its eye and asserting dominance before starting the attack run.

Some stock dogs are more powerful than others and can control livestock from a greater distance. That is an advantage for the same reason that a long lever is better than a short one. Thirty feet out, the shift of a powerful dog's head can alter a flock's direction. Nearer, the dog has to run from one side of the sheep to the other, unsettling them.

When sheep ignore him, Pip comes in too close. When they defy him, he takes it personally and is quick to nip. When a dog bites (grips) a sheep on the trial field, he is disqualified.

Pip has good points, too. He has good balance and thinks well for himself. If you need a dog to fetch sheep out of a thicket, Pip's the dog to send. Wait around a bit and, directly, he'll bring them to you.

Pip is dead honest. You can read it in his eyes.

* * *

Dog trialing is an amateur sport. Purses aren't great, and trials are often far apart. Not too many men are willing to drive a thousand miles with their dogs to run ten minutes on a trial course for a top prize of $750. Those few men do know dogs. They give training clinics, sell pups, import dogs, train dogs for others, put on demonstrations at state fairs and agricultural exhibitions, and put forty thousand miles a year on their pickups.

Since many successful trial dogs are imported, already trained, from Scotland, a Scots dialect is commonly used for dog commands. It is bizarre to see a broad-chested American rancher—in boots, a Western shirt, enormous Stetson—waving a Scottish shepherd's crook and urging his dog to "Lie doon, Mon. Laadie, lie doon."

The Big Hats—that's what the top handlers are called.

Ralph Pulfer has been running dogs for twenty-five years. By his own count, he has imported better than two hundred dogs. I doubt he's counted his trial trophies—he has a room full of them. Ralph is a formidable competitor and has twice won the Grand National Championship. Although Ralph always brings a couple of dogs to run, his top dog is the classic seven-year-old Shep. Shep is a biddable dog—extremely responsive to commands. He was winning trials before I bought my first Border collie.

Lewis Pulfer, Ralph's brother, is a soft-spoken, articulate man and a very stylish handler. His red bitch, Dell, has won many trials and is the dam of several champions. Dell often finds her daughters and granddaughters competing against her.

This year, Lewis is trialing Moss, a powerful dog—energetic and a trifle hardheaded.

Bruce Fogt and Tom Conn are among the best young handlers. Bruce has won the Kentucky Blue

Grass, the Blue Ridge Open, and the California State Fair. Bruce trained his Hope bitch himself, and she's a wonder to watch. She's a medium-size, black-and-merle bitch, strong, responsive, smooth as glass. Tom Conn is running Rod, who won the BBC television trials before coming to the States. These televised trials, "One Man and His Dog," have been enormously popular in Britain. They'd seem funky and peculiar to most Americans, but Americans are often uneasy around dogs.

Jack Knox has trained more dog handlers than anyone, traveling every year from Michigan to Alabama, Oregon to Maryland, teaching beginners how to work their dogs. Jack is running his nine-year-old Jan bitch and Hope, his six-year-old male.

And there's Stan Moore with Midge, Bill Wyatt with Cap, John Bauserman with Bess, Joe Lawson with Drift, and Ethel Conrad with Tess. I love to watch them run the open course. They make it look so easy.

I have a writer's concentration, intense but flickering. This concentration is useful writing about dogs; less so when trialing them. Going blank for ten seconds won't wreck an essay, but is disastrous with sheep coming on like the express and your dog slewing about like a drunk.

Too often I substitute will for sensitivity. I'm a man whose second thoughts are better than his first.

As a team Pip and I are uneven. At our best, we can tiptoe a dozen spooky rams alongside the unfenced border of my wife's vegetable garden. At our worst, I blue the air with bellowing while Pip grabs some desperate sheep by the wool and won't turn loose.

A sheepdog trial is the most difficult test of a man and dog ever divised. Tubs of cool water are kept at the end of the course because, after just ten minutes of running a trial, the dogs need that water to drop their body temperatures back to normal. Many good farm dogs have come to grief on a trial course. It's the difference, you see, between racing at Indianapolis and driving Aunt Millie to the airport.

The *outrun* is three-hundred-plus yards. The *lift* is the first moment of contact between the dog and his sheep, when they read each other. The dog *fetches* the sheep to his handler's feet. Then, he pushes them away through several freestanding gates (the *drive*). Finally, man and dog press the sheep into a six-by-nine-foot *pen*. At most trials the dog then takes one sheep off from the others, the *shed*, but there'll be no shed at the Blue Ridge Open. It's just too hot. Time limit: ten minutes.

Judges deduct points for overcommanding, under-commanding, going off line, wobbling, losing contact with the sheep, circling the pen, and numerous other sins. Good runs are characterized by respect: sheep for dog, dog for man, man for dog and sheep. Good runs are smooth and quiet. When respect breaks down, things go to hell in a hurry.

The Blue Ridge Open Sheepdog Trial is held in May near White Post, Virginia, an hour southwest of Washington, D.C. It's a two-day trial of the first rank: strong sponsorship, a challenging course, and a Scottish judge. Each dog runs twice for a cumulative score. Dogs and handlers come here from Michigan, New York, Pennsylvania, Georgia, Tennessee, and Ohio. The Big Hats are coming.

Late Friday night, the nearest motel is already full with Border Collies and their owners. On the lawn, handlers stand about swapping lies while their dogs strut around, tails erect, observing dog rituals.

When we go inside, Pip jumps up on the other bed and gives me a look. His eyes are whirling, Betty Boop eyes. After all, he is another species—his mind unfathomable.

Next morning I don't bother with breakfast, and he doesn't eat anything either. On the way to the trial grounds, he rides up on the front seat. I'd like to listen to Bruce Springsteen, but Pip doesn't care for rock 'n' roll.

Spring is further along here than home. I see where one farmer's already mowed his first cutting of alfalfa. Another has put up his winter rye in great green round bales. Round bales look wonderful fresh and so dumpy and awful old.

This is the fringe of Virginia's horse country. The farms are working farms, but most have wooden jumps built over their woven-wire fences so the Hunt can ride through.

Sunnybrook Farm is a livestock farm. There's a big red wooden barn with stalls underneath, a modern tenant house, freshly painted white with green trim. The high-tensile fences are taut, straight as a die. The road climbs through the farm onto a high lush pasture. Bluegrass and orchard grass and clumps of trees for shade. A young girl at the gate is collecting a dollar from spectators. If this is like most trials, there won't be many.

Campers, vans, and pickups are lined up behind the course. Lawn chairs and coolers overlook the field. The judge's booth is a horse trailer. Novice dogs started running at 7:30 A.M., and the judge will work until 6:00 P.M. when the last of the dogs make their try.

I say a few hellos, shake a few hands. On the course a young dog is in trouble, his handler's commands unheeded. Sheep can read an inexperienced dog, and this one can't do a thing with them. The sheep bolt off the course, and the dog and handler are disqualified.

The novice dogs and handlers are listed on the scoreboard. Hell, novice is where Pip and I *belong*.

Sheepdog trialing is a farmer's sport, so talk is about crops and weather, markets, sheep, cattle, and dogs—always dogs. "Haven't seen you since the Alabama Trial. How's that Mirk dog of yours?"

Pip tugs at the lead, eager to sniff other dogs' signs.

I take this as a bad sign—a sign that Pip's insufficiently serious.

There's a quiet locust grove behind the course where it'll stay shady as the sun moves across the day. When I tie Pip, he sighs and flops down.

I'm scheduled to run seventh, Open Class, after Ethel Conrad and her Tess. Last year Tess won more trials than any other dog in Virginia. Ethel was invited to the David Letterman show, where Tess herded ducks with perfect aplomb despite Letterman's attempts to turn her into a joke. Tess has worked sheep on the Capitol Mall before the secretary of agriculture. Oh boy.

There are men here who run a thousand sheep and cows. I chat with a woman who's looking to buy three sheep so she can work her dog. Some of the handlers never got past eighth grade; others have Ph.D.s. Their dogs are more uniform: All are well schooled.

You could probably buy some of the novice dogs for less than $1,000. One addled young dog grips his sheep at the pen and is disqualified, and his irritated handler marches off the course. Right now, you might get that dog pretty cheap. Open dogs go for $2,500 and up. And up. Last year, Ralph Pulfer sold his Nan bitch for $8,000.

The judge, Viv Billingham, is a slender blond woman with sun lines at the corners of her eyes. Viv and her husband Geoff shepherd 750 ewes on the duke of Roxburgh's estate in the Cheviot Hills (the Scottish Borders). With her bluff, powerful dog Garry, Viv has twice made the Scottish National Team. We Americans have watched her and Garry on tapes of "One Man and His Dog."

Ralph Pulfer arrived at the Blue Ridge Trial a couple of days early to teach this woman judge a thing or two about the fine points of judging an American trial. I gather he ruffled Viv Billingham's feathers.

Scottish trial men are often invited to judge the

bigger American trials. For the judge it's an inexpensive (if rather doggy) American holiday. Their hosts get a few private tips, a familiar voice when they phone up the UK wanting a dog—as well as somebody to score eighty dogs from sunup to sundown, attentive to each one.

Usually a judge will work several trials, the hosts splitting expenses and airfare, but Viv is the very first woman judge ever invited "to cross the water" and some of the good old boys didn't want to be judged by a woman, no matter how able, so Viv will only judge the Blue Ridge and later in the week will give a training clinic to defray expenses.

She's never worked in a training ring before and says, "The only proper training for a sheepdog is the Hill," but is so pleased working the young dogs she soon gets the hang of it. Many novice dog handlers own dogs that are better bred than they are trained. Most go back to this or that imported trial winner who will, like as not, be the son or daughter of an International Champion. Thus, the dogs Viv sees here are grandsons and granddaughters of the dogs she knows in Scotland, and as each dog comes into the ring she says, "Oh, dear, Dryden Joe?" or "Fortune's Glen?" or "Willie Welch's Don? He must be. Does he have a tendency to run a bit too wide, out of contact with his sheep?"

And often she'll describe a dog's character before it does any work at all, because she's seen its grandsire or granddam run in trials. "He'll be a little sulky then, won't take correction?" "Tell me, does he turn his head back to you, looking for instructions? Keeking, we call it. Oh, his sire was a terrible keeker."

It is politically unpopular to claim that human character traits (intelligence, courage, ingenuity) can be inherited. But that's the working belief in the sheepdog breeding world. It is thought that a dog sired by Wiston Cap, one who looks like the old man, will likely behave like his eminent sire.

In various human cultures, it was believed that the same applied to human rulers, that "blood would tell." Alas, not many British dukes are bred as closely as his poorest shepherd's dogs. Even fewer dukes are bred for accomplishment.

What is likely true about dogs is unlikely with men.

What the British noted about their dogs, they attributed to their kings.

Viv Billingham judges by Scottish standards, which are quite rigorous. If your sheep go off course, you're disqualified. If your dog grips, you're disqualified. If you fail to pen your sheep and don't complete the course, you're disqualified. The scorekeeper writes "DQ" after another novice dog's name. DQ—that's the score most novices have.

I wander back to the course to visit with the pit crew—the men putting out sheep, three at a time, all day long. By day's end they'll be sunburned, bone weary, and stinking of sheep. Last year I worked back here.

Somebody wishes me good luck.

From here it's easier to see things from the dog's point of view. The dog sails out, out, and cannot see the sheep until he's almost on top of them. The instant the dog loses faith in himself or his handler, he's lost, and many young dogs get in trouble today. Out here, a handler's commands are almost inaudible, and whistles are fainter than bird calls.

The good dogs glide toward their sheep, ignoring the workers, the pickup trucks and trailers. The sheep drift down the course with the dog on their heels.

Ralph Pulfer steps up. He's first to run in Open Class with his four-year-old bitch, Maid.

My stomach feels like I've swallowed a brick.

When I go back to Pip, he wriggles gladness. I sit beside him to calm him, but he's calmer than I am.

"What's so different about today, Boss? We go out, get sheep, pop them in the pen, right?"

Right.

I walk him to loosen him up and give him a chance to void himself. He has a fine time, sniffing and peeing on every bush where other dogs have passed—quite the model of the stud Border Collie. Right now, I'd rather have a worker than a lover.

I bring him to the edge of the course to watch another dog's lift. When the sheep come out of the release pen, I say, "See sheep? See sheep?"

You bet he does.

My own big hat came from Houston, Texas, and a cowboy pal of mine gave me the silver concho hatband. I wear it for weddings, funerals, and sheepdog trials.

As we wait I try to find my own center, but it eludes me. It seems very hot, and Pip scoots under the truck next to me. At the time, I thought he was just seeking shade, but later I realized he was afraid.

The announcer calls my name, does some sort of introduction about my being a writer and so on. I don't hear much of it. With Pip at my side I step onto the course. Until the dog brings the sheep to the pen, the handler must stay at the handler's stake. If he leaves and goes to help his dog, he'll be disqualified.

I stand Pip beside my left leg, and though my mouth is dry, I manage to send him out. Pip's quick, and he flies out in a fine, plain outrun. When he disappears in a dip, I put the whistle to my mouth to redirect him, but no need, he comes out fine, right on target.

The big hat is awful damn heavy.

Pip sails up nice behind his sheep but stops thirty yards short. Since you lose fewer points redirecting your dog than letting him persist in his mistake, I shout, "Get back!" and whistle him on. Thank God, he takes my commands, and the sheep come hell-for-leather. The fetch line is supposed to be straight, but no time to worry about that now, worry about Pip pushing them beyond me and off course. I command Pip to "Stand," but he keeps on coming, full tilt. "Stand," "Stand there!" "Pip! Lie down!"

The sheep sail on, heedless, intent (I fear) on racing off course, and for our score: DQ—a fat zero. Too soon I flank him around, just as the sheep are slowing short of the handler's stake. I look at the sheep, they look at me. They're half tame, accustomed to men and dogs.

Pip's where he should be to start the drive, but he has arrived five seconds early, and the sheep turn below me instead of above. There'll be points gone for that. The drive isn't too bad—a little jerky—and the sheep go right through the panel, just like they should but, once more, I flank Pip too early, and he drives them back the way they'd come, undoing all the good he'd done. The sheep start across the course but break into a run, and I go blank. Pip stops and looks at me. "What now, Boss? What's the plan?"

When they are three-quarters the way to the final gates, I hook him around and, once again, Pip gets there faster than I had expected and turns the sheep before they have had a chance to go through the gates.

The three sheep are panting as they come up the hill toward me and the pen. Pip's tongue is hanging out a yard.

We must get them penned. No pen, no points. There's a line attached to the gate, and I wrap it tight around my hand. The sheep come on, Pip lies down, and the sheep are coming straight at me, ignoring the yawning gate of the pen. Now what? *Now what?*

Once sheep start circling a pen, you start losing points, and it gets much harder to get them inside. The handler can't touch the sheep at the pen, but it's okay if they run into him. I drop into a goalie crouch right in front of the sheep. We are eyeball to eyeball, and I hiss at them like a furious goose.

"Pip, get back!" Wonder of wonders, Pip does as

he's bid, and with the pressure relieved, the sheep slip into the pen and I bang the gate shut behind them.

Pip is panting hard, and his eyes are wide. When he flops in the water tub, I slosh water over his back and neck. Already the next handler is at the stake, and his dog is running. I can hear the whistles.

As the day wears on, the Big Hats post scores in the sixties and seventies. Pip and I have 48 points.

We do beat Ralph Pulfer and Shep, but we haven't earned the victory. The Scottish judge has just taught the American expert a lesson in manners.

When Pip's feeling better, I park him in the shade. "We fared right common, didn't we partner?" He gives me a look. He doesn't need me to know how badly we did.

There's a handler's supper at Sunnybrook after everybody runs, so I return to the motel to clean up. I'm peeved at Pip for the short outrun. En route, I play Bruce Springsteen. Loud as I like.

The farmhouse at Sunnybrook is a big, rambling sort of place. Most handlers eat outside on the porch. Stan Moore and Lewis Pulfer have had good runs and are pleased and modest. Some who have done poorly blame their dog or the judge. Most of the Big Hats talk about other trials, other runs.

American handlers are eager to hear about doings in Scotland, and in the dining room, Viv Billingham holds court. Viv describes eminent dogs: Wiston Cap, Wilson's Cap, McTeir's Ben, Fingland Loos, Wilson's Roy, Richardson's Mirk, and Sweep . . . and the shepherds who showed these dogs their life's work and enjoyed a man/dog conversation of subtlety and power. Viv speaks about last year's International, the most important sheepdog trial in the world, where, on the final day, the dog works so terribly far from his shepherd. She tells us about men we know only because we've seen the dogs they've exported. We rich Americans are as curious about poor shepherds and their dogs as soap opera fans are about the stars of their favorite shows. We want to know everything. Of her own success, Viv says only, "Over there they say Garry made me. I don't mind them saying it. I owe Garry more than I can ever pay."

She also says, "It takes great courage for a dog to get out there and do his best before strangers. When a handler does a poor job, he makes a fool of his dog. Don't think the dog doesn't know it."

Later, outside, handlers describe good runs and joke about spectacularly bad ones. Wives chat. Kids play together. A big smiling handler starts to tell how his Missy dog wandered onto the highway, but he can't finish and turns away so nobody can see his tears.

Later, they show a videotape of "One Man and His Dog" in the living room. Still later, when most folks have gone off to bed, you can hear a couple of disappointed handlers, drunk, still working their dogs down by the old red barn.

Back at the motel, when I cut my car lights, Pip's face is peering through the curtains, waiting.

The second day of the trials they changed the running order, but it made no difference to me and Pip. When I brought him out on the course, he crouched like a feral creature, a fox caught suddenly in the headlights, and it was trouble the moment I set him off. I lacked confidence in him and he in me. Soon he decided to take matters into his own hands. I wrestled him around the course with shouts and bellows. Twice he tried to nip, but both times I shouted him off. We avoided DQ, by a hair. After the pen, he was so disgusted he didn't wait for me but took off for the cooling tubs on his own.

As the final runs were made, clouds were building in the east. Stan Moore slipped in the standings. Lewis Pulfer and Moss turned in an elegant run. Lewis's whistles were so quiet I wondered Moss could hear them.

Afterward, the handlers and dogs gathered while Viv Billingham awarded trophies. First: Lewis Pulfer with Moss. Second: Bruce Fogt and Hope. Third: Tom Conn with Rod. Of forty entries, Pip and I were twenty-fifth. Dogs sniffed their sniffs. Handlers made plans for trials farther down the road.

Before I got in the car, I spoke to the judge. She said, "Yesterday, when that dog of yours seemed to be stopping short on the outrun, he wasn't short. He was correct. The sheep were facing him, you see, and if you hadn't shouted him on, they would have lifted off straight and easy."

Oh.

It was raining pretty hard by the time we hit the interstate. Rain drummed on the roof of the car, and Pip lay on the front seat, his head turned to the door.

"Better luck next time," I said.

Pip was so mad he wouldn't look at me. He wouldn't meet my eyes for three days.

2

The Only Proper Training
for a Sheepdog
Is the Hill

Three of the next four winters were mild. Thanks to my wife's hard work, our sheep flock flourished. I renovated an old orchard, and that year our firewood was aromatic of apple trees planted before I was born. I replaced the rotting timbers under our barn with new twelve-by-twelves. Pip and I got older. I decided to go to Scotland.

I was incurious about the place.

Many Americans boast about their Scottish roots, trace genealogical connections to this savage sept, that barbarous clan. In summer months, crowds of Americans travel hundreds of miles to gather in some hot meadow with like-minded souls for Scottish games: ox-shaped worthies heaving immature telephone poles, folk dancers prancing nervously around claymores (the swords Scots used after more sensible fighters switched to firearms), and amateur bagpipers cater-wauling. Some Americans, I am told, don kilts for these festive gatherings.

The Scots do make good whisky. In Bobby Burns, they had a great poet, but I've never drunk enough whisky to understand him. They breed and train the best sheepdogs in the world.

My father's father was a Scottish Catholic, a granite cutter and IWW radical who was middle aged when he contracted silicosis. As he weakened, he scooted his wife and three kids from kin to kin across the High Line (the United States–Canadian border). He'd park his family with more prosperous relatives while he looked for work. ("Just until spring, Jess. In the spring, you'll all have to go.")

The richer kinfolks lost patience quicker than the poor ones did, and during my grandfather's last months, the family squatted with his wife's sister on a hardscrabble waterless homestead carved out of a Montana Indian reservation. To his dying day my father hated potatoes. That winter, potatoes were what they'd had to eat.

In 1971, when I quit my advertising job in New York City and moved to a rundown Appalachian farm, my father was sick about it. After all, he'd boosted his family into the middle class, given both his kids college educations. I suppose he'd thought us safe, a long way from that dirt-roof soddy and the bitter smell of the other people's laundry his mother had to wash.

"Why," my father asked, "are you throwing it all away?"

In my father's papers, after his death, I found a letter he'd written when he was a boy. It was directed to his mother's mother, who had a small house in Great Falls.

Millet, Alta.
Aug. 30, 1915

Dear Grandma,
 School starts today but Bob and I aren't
going. I will be glad when we leave this place
and see papa. We pray for you every night. We
are going to have a surprise party on Bob for his
birthday. We have went to two children's
parties. I wish you were with us.
 Your loving grandson,
 Donald McCaig

The boy's letter was written on the back of a letter his
father had written to his wife. Since, inevitably, both letters would be seen by the grandmother, it's hard to puzzle
out the dynamic. Presumably, the boy's mother wanted
the grandmother to know how desperate they were.

 give her no chance to refuse. I wish we could get
 to Denver this fall then I could work and you
 keep house. Don't fret about Alice. [His sister,
 Alice, had a state job in Denver.] Your going to
 Denver will never put her in bankruptcy and she
 writes a good many of those hard luck letters. I
 think mamma so you won't expect anything of
 her. I don't doubt she has been sick but she can't
 get along for ½ year on nothing and you wont
 cost her any thing and if I don't get that far
 there are lots of ways you could help her. and
 she knows it.

No biographers puzzle over the strategies that
characterized these unsuccessful lives. My family was
too poor to be interesting. The McCaigs came to Canada sometime before 1840. I figured: If this hell was
what they immigrated *to,* what hell was Scotland,
where they'd emigrated *from?*

Our farm was lovely that February. We had extra
cords of firewood and the pipes didn't freeze. Though

it stayed fairly cold, we had only light dustings of snow. The farm lies between the Shenandoah and Bull Pasture mountains and they're steep enough you can't see their tops unless you're standing in our frozen hay-fields in the middle of the valley. Our near neighbors are two miles down the valley, and on frosty mornings, I'd hear their coon dogs yelp.

But sometimes, as I walked through the stick trees of the winter orchard, I'd be discontented. Those foot-prints in the snow: those were Pip's; those, the rabbit's who lived under the brushpile; those, my own, made just yesterday. I'd wave at a neighbor driving by: Red Wright. I remembered when Red bought that blue Chevrolet.

At eight years old, Pip was getting past it. The dog who'd once been too quick needed cunning to catch young ewes. The dog who'd jumped every fence on the farm now waited patiently for me to open gates for him.

Me, I'd got older and just wiser enough so it hurt. I'd made stupid, willful mistakes training Pip and my blunders showed every time Pip ran out on the trial field. Because I'd urgently wanted control of a keen young dog, I'd downed him each time I was un-sure and destroyed his natural rhythm, created that clappiness that upset the sheep. I'd trained his flanks ("Go right, go left") in a big field without *sheep*. Con-sequently, now, when I asked him to make a "blind" outrun—no sheep in sight—he wouldn't: He circles my legs, anger and confusion warring in his brown eyes.

The miracle is that Pip worked at all—that we had any instants of clarity. With a better trainer he would have made one hell of a sheepdog.

I was like a middle-aged man, looking back at my marriage, knowing I could not undo what I had done, not the least part of it, yearning for the impossible: to start over fresh.

I thought to make a pilgrimage. Three months in a foreign land, filled with dog trainers whose routine work is completely beyond anything we can do here in the States. Shepherds and farmers who somehow create dogs who are achingly beautiful. I would sit at their feet. I would find a young bitch and bring her back with me. I would begin again.

I wrote Viv Billingham: How are things?

I hear you quit the duke of Roxburgh and moved to a new place. Do you like it? How's husband, Geoff? Geoff, Junior? Are there any good young bitches for sale? I'm coming over in April.

Viv never answered. I wrote to Barbara Carpenter, president of the British Border Collie Club. She wrote back: Pastor's Hill House lay between London and Scotland and she'd welcome a visit.

I should probably add that I'm a terrible traveler: don't care for airports, airplanes, unfamiliar roads. Away from home I get fretful and discouraged. I hate to be a stranger.

Friday, April 23, 6:35 P.M. Greenwich time, a travel-goofy, nervous American honked out of Heathrow Airport in a red Ford Fiesta that had its steering wheel and gearshift lever on the wrong side. My luggage rode in the back seat, heaped in the clamshell halves of the dog kennel I hoped my young bitch would use, if and when I found her.

My prayer: I'd know her when I saw her. I had a thousand pounds to spend and three months to search Scotland before my wife wearied of caring for a 300-acre farm and 150 ewes without my help. That night, on the M3 motorway, my wife seemed close. So did the hospital.

That Friday was a bank holiday and, in Britain, when banks go on holiday, everybody else goes too. The motorway was bumper to bumper with merry souls. I cowered in the far left lane among the grocers' lorries and caravans (travel trailers), while bolder motorists jetted by on the right at ninety and a hundred miles an hour. Britons are an extraordinarily warlike people. Hell, they conquered most of the world. Why did I expect namby-pambies on the motorway? Big, smooth sports cars passed me. Junkers, crammed with drunk kids, passed, too. If my great grandmother hadn't been dead, no doubt she'd have passed as well.

From time to time there'd be a police pulloff, but I never once saw a cop. Perhaps the police go on holiday along with everybody else. It was a jolly throng.

Blurry with jet lag, I anguished over the simplest decisions: Time to stop for gas? Dare I chance a faster lane? American diplomats frequently brag of visiting four countries in as many days while enacting treaties that affect life and death. Henry Kissinger nicknamed his jetlag "Shuttle Diplomacy."

It got gray, then dark. The traffic thinned as holidaymakers peeled off for their rural retreats. Across the Severn River Bridge, I exited the motorway into black countryside. Briefly the road was two lanes before it shrank to one lane and shriveled further. Tremendous trees edged closer to the road until they clamped fast with thick overhead branches interlaced against the night sky. Brute stone walls shouldered into the verge. The road adopted a six-inch curb, which I'd smack every time I met oncoming traffic. I'd strike, bounce into the air, and barely regain control. No, I'd told the car-rental girl, I didn't want the optional collision insurance.

"But it's just two pounds, seventy a day, sir."

Farmhouses, dark. Villages, dark. I supposed, if I lost the faint thread of Mrs. Carpenter's directions, I could sleep in the car. I'd hate that.

The streets in Bream were plenty wide for a horse and rider, even a fat horse and rider. I squiggled between stone buildings, figuring that if my right-hand mirror didn't get knocked off, my left mirror could take care of itself. I comforted myself that no other car had ever got stuck. If a car had got stuck, it'd still be here.

Pastor's Hill House is a two-story Jacobean stone farmhouse on eighty grassy acres. Stone outbuildings, slate roofs, stone workpens.

I didn't see all that when I got out and stretched. The car ticked. Fluids gurgled. Metal shrank and cooled. For the first time I sniffed the spring English countryside. It was a dank, luxuriant smell—attar of roses. Overhead, the chilly stars winked. But these were British stars. Dogs cried out, "INTRUDER, IN-TRUDER!"

"Oh hush now, you, Tag, hush."

Straightaway Barbara Carpenter led me into her home, through the kitchen, into the siting room, with its table, two plump chairs by the fire, and a couch (which Border Collies had appropriated). Two dogs came over to say hello. The others decided to wait a bit. "I hope you haven't eaten," she said, pouring a cup of strong tea. "It's just stew." Chunks of beef, carrots, onions, potatoes. What is good over here is good over there. I was back in dog land and, suddenly, sleepily, everything was all right.

Since the British aristocracy was selected for war skills, and since hunting approximates those skills, and since writers eat by praising the rich ("Old King Olaf is a mighty King, flattens his foes with his pinky ring"), there is a considerable literature on sporting dogs. Border Collies, the dogs of poor, frequently illiterate shepherds, have been rarely sung. Though Samuel Pepys noticed them, it wasn't until 1829 that anyone (James Hogg in *A Shepherd's Calendar*) wrote anything memorable about them. Collections of sheepdog books make a scruffy library: Government pamphlets issued by the Queensland Agricultural Board (*Practical Cattle and Sheepdog Training*) vie for space with skinny privately printed tracts (*Ten Thousand Dogs, The Sheep-dog in South Africa*) and a few hardcover books from agricultural presses that, on the back flap, offer their backlist books on "stick dressing," "laying of proper hedgerows," "building and maintenance of the dry-stane wall." Barbara Carpenter has a grand collection. She also has scrapbooks, ISDS (International Sheep-dog Society) studbooks, photographs and slides of dog men and great dogs, and jumpy home movies of J. M. Wilson with Ben and Jock Richardson with Sweep.

She'd say, "I hope all this isn't boring you."

"I'll have a little more tea if it's hot."

Barbara Carpenter's a sixtyish, shy, happily obsessed farm woman who was putting together a photo book of all the dogs who'd won the International Sheepdog Trial since 1906. She wrote letters, imploring—begging—descendants to search one more time through granddad's trunk.

"Oh, aye, I remember Granddad speaking about a dog—Kep, was it? Sweep?"

Mrs. Carpenter's small flock of Welsh mountain sheep was in good bloom except for one young ewe who'd suffered a back injury. Daily, Barbara Carpenter got the ewe onto her feet (physical therapy), and once a week she'd lift her into the station wagon and haul her twenty miles to the chiropractor. She's got a dozen dogs: trial dogs, retired trial dogs, dogs that never quite made the grade. "Oh I couldn't sell Lynn. They'd find out what a terrible coward she is and they'd lose their temper, and it's not her fault" (with a pat). "She can't help it that she's afraid."

Bob spent all his waking moments pressed to the crack in the sitting room door, hoping for a glimpse of the cats. Donald haunted Chip's heels, hoping for an excuse for a fight. Chip and Tag and Tash were Barbara's trial dogs.

We walked the farm, worked dogs, talked. She talked about Jon, the dog she'd inherited in 1978 when her husband Will died. Jon was a hard sort of dog with a merle face and a black patch over one eye. "Quite raffish, Jon was. He sort of, well, took over when Will died. I don't know what I would have done without him." As Will's funeral party was leaving the grave-yard, a dog man slipped up to her elbow and offered to buy Jon, and she thought, "If I was going to sell Jon, I wouldn't sell him to you." She'd never had a dog sleep in her bedroom before but, a woman deep in the coun-try, widowed, newly alone. . . . During the night, if something was wrong—a car parked by the gate, some fox worrying the sheep—Jon'd reach out and touch her cheek with his paw, just a touch.

Of course she trialed him, or tried to. She laughed, "Sometimes we were together—other times"—(she shook her head). "One trial had a right-hand cross-drive, and John drove them all the way across and then turned and drove them all the way back again, despite my shouts. How I shouted. Oh, Jon had his head down. He heard me all right. 'Well, Bugger her,' he said. We were the second to last dog to run, and afterwards the judge came up and asked how I was, and I said I was bloody furious. 'Well yes,' the judge said."

Most men have only one great dog in a lifetime. After Lyr Evan's Coon died, Lyr was never any use on the trial field. John Angus McLeod still talks about Ben as if Ben were alive. When Thompson McKnight's Drift died, Thompson gave up trialing.

Such bright memories. In May when I asked Jock Richardson about his great dog Wiston Cap, Jock shook his slow head, "I can see him running yet in my mind," he said, "I just canna explain it."

I asked Barbara Carpenter if the Scots had the best dogs. "They'll tell you so," she said. "They're certainly the dearest."

I wasn't the first American to come to Britain to look for a dog. Every year, the National and International Trials have their contingents of Yanks making notes in their programs, dogging the great handlers, chasing rumors of a great dog the length of the island.

There've been good Border Collies in the States since the Civil War. Some came to work the vast ranches British syndicates were building in the American West, with British livestock worked by British dogs. Sometimes Scottish immigrants would bring over a favorite dog to use on their new homesteads. There are reports of Border Collies driving turkeys down the peninsula to San Francisco for the Christmas holidays of 1879, and I've photographs of Border Collies in Montana sheep camps in the 1880s. America no long imports Angus or Hereford cattle. We no longer import Cheviot or Suffolk or Dorset sheep. But every year, we cross the ocean for Border Collies.

The very first people in America who could handle the dogs were Scots like Sam Stoddart, who'd handled them in his native land. American farmers and stockmen had never seen anything like these dogs, and, in fact, would pay money to see them work. Men like Stoddart and, later, Arthur Allen, made the circuit of state fairs, livestock exhibitions, and rodeos (Allen and his dogs were regulars for many years with the Roy Rogers Show). A handful of Americans knew how to train and handle the Border Collie. They were making a living from their knowledge and, with only a few exceptions (Lewis Pence, Pope Robertson), they didn't share their knowledge.

And Americans, who train horses as well as anyone, breed sheep, cattle, and hogs among the best in the world, are appallingly ignorant about dogs. Pick up any veterinary supplies catalog, turn to the dog section: Count the shock collars. *Shock collars?*

As Americans became increasingly urban, they lost touch with animals familiar to earlier generations, and as two-worker households became the norm, the dog population dwindled. Thanks to televised nature shows many American children know more about whales and Bengal tigers than they know about man's best friend.

Suppose you were a stockman who saw Stoddart or Allen with their wonderful dogs and maybe you bought a pup. Sometime after those gents left town, after the pup was half grown, you took the pup out to your sheep and said, "Shep, fetch," and sure enough, Shep took off like a streak and gathered the sheep but what he did then was run around them in circles, nipping and pulling wool; and Shep, who until that moment had been the smartest, most obedient dog you'd ever seen, wouldn't listen to a word you said. What would you do then? Many stockmen shot the dog.

Of a Border Collie litter of six puppies, five will work stock. Of twenty young "started" dogs, perhaps one will be good enough to trial. Of sixty trial dogs, one can win a local trial. A couple of wins will qualify him for the Scottish, English, Welsh, or Irish National Trials, where eight hundred trial winners are winnowed to a team of fifteen dogs per nation. (Ireland has only ten dogs.) Of the fifty-five dogs that run in the International, only one is the supreme champion. The oldest champion was J. J. McKnight's Gael, at 10½ years. The youngest was Telfer's Midge at 13 months.

There is no way to pick an International winner from a litter of pups. Until the pups see sheep, at six months of age, there's no way to know which will work at all. Border Collie pups are cheap: 80 to 90 pounds. You can't buy an International winner. John Templeton's Roy has earned 10,000 pounds in prize money and stud fees.

For hill shepherds, whose income runs to 400 pounds a month, starting and training sheep dogs is a grand way to put extra jam on the table. Many sell a dog every year. Others use their dogs until they're three or four before they replace them with younger ones. They'll take a new dog to the Hill (with a couple experienced dogs for backup), using the young dog as his skills increase. A trained hill dog will finally be able to gather eight hundred ewes scattered over two or three thousand acres. He will be able to work by himself or to whistled commands at distances of a mile or more. He can run a hundred miles Thursday and get up Friday morning and do it again.

Since the dogs are trained by real work, training is never a quantity business. Each dog is trained individually, and each takes time and attention.

The best dogs are scarce and sought after. The trial men want them, and dog dealers want them. Every week, buyers like Peter Hetherington are on the phone. "Have you heard of a strong dog? Two year old? For Texas."

Again, I asked Barbara Carpenter: "Are the Scottish dogs really best?"

Barbara remembered a dog Bob James bought for the trials. One day the dog would work beautifully, but at the next trial he'd sulk and dive in at his sheep and refuse commands. James phoned the dog's trainer: What was the trouble here?

Ever afterwards, just before the dog stepped onto the trial course, Bob James brought it a wee tot of whiskey. After the dog lapped it up he ran fine. "Of course," Barbara Carpenter said slyly, "He was a Scottish dog."

Sunday afternoon. After lush Gloucestershire, the Scottish Borders were charmless: cold, barren, hard. Some of the rubble heaps on the sere hills might have been castles at one time, but they were definitely rubble heaps now. A sign outside Moffat boasted that it was the "Best Kept Small Village in Scotland." The British commonly tour in coaches (buses), and coaches were bumper to bumper around the town square. Holidayers strolled the town inspecting wool shops and gewgaw shops ("See our collection of single malts"), and a tinny loudspeaker squeaked bagpipe tunes of love and death at plump tourists placidly chewing toffees. The sky was overcast, dull. One of Moffat's hotels is the world's narrowest, listed in the *Guinness Book of World Records*. The only statue in the town square is a statue of a sheep. One day, perhaps Moffat will erect one to the tourist, who is much easier to shear.

Hands in pockets, I moped through the Moffat graveyard. Tall, spikey, red stones; part marker, part lance. A fair number of stones were for Scots who had "died in America." I knew I should think about this, it disturbed me, but I didn't know how.

I telephoned Viv Billingham.

"Oh yes, Donald. Glad you made it all right. I'm sorry I didn't answer your letter, but it came late and you'd be here soon anyway. Oh it's a jumble at Tweedhope. Builders, you see."

I asked if there were any B & Bs nearby, and Viv said she was sorry but the accommodations at Tweedhope weren't finished yet and there was nothing in Tweedsmuir; but surely there was something in Moffat.

"Do come by and see us, Donald," she added. Uh-huh.

I was up at dawn and unbolted the narrow wooden doors of the respectable guesthouse and hiked down to the square. No coaches. All the rubbish bins were overflowing, but the garbage men were working at it. The few souls on the streets all seemed to know each other. I killed time. The newsagent opened. I bought a tabloid and read about heartbreak and fury. Drank coffee. Ate a scone. Asked where I could find a laundromat. Someone thought, perhaps, Dunfries. The butcher shop had homemade sausages and thick cut bacon and advertised: "Scottish Beef." The grocer had few canned or frozen vegetables and only taties and onions fresh.

Among the tourist brochures at my guesthouse (*Scotland's Whiskey Tour, Guided Hillwalks*) was one for the Billinghams' place: *Tweedhope Border Collie and Shepherding Centre.* It had a nice photograph of Viv's Garry and Laddie.

Outside Moffat, the road steepened as it climbed the side of the Devil's Beeftub. That's what they named the vast bowl when Border rustlers used to store stolen cattle there. It would have held several million. The Beeftub was big enough to have fog in the bottom, clouds obscuring the top, and enough blue sky in between for a Sunday picnic.

Drystane dykes (walls) clambered slopes so steep it would have been tough to stand upright let alone lay an eighty-pound stone in place. What men had done this work?

On top, the hills blurred under ranks of young spruce, deep and featureless, blackish green. Other hills were furrowed, like a giant child had dragged his fingers down them, and puny trees shivered in those furrows. Road signs noted points of historical interest, at present swallowed by trees.

The Billinghams' place is the first human habitation on the downslope, a scattering of stone buildings on both banks of the headwaters of the River Tweed. It has the feel of a roadhouse on a high pass in America's Rocky Mountains. The Billinghams have a hundred acres along the stream, hemmed in by the road on one side, impenetrable dark woods on the other.

Vanloads of workmen were hard at it. One crew was gutting the old drover's inn, a taciturn young man was laying a drystane abutment below Tweedhope's parking area, the district council had started (but not completed) a coach layby (roadside pulloff).

The lane was prettily landscaped. The heavy heads of yellow crocuses bent to the chill breeze.

Geoff Billingham's a soft spoken, tallish artistic man, distinguished enough for a whisky ad. The Dewar's White Label ad showed Geoff with his team of brace bitches at his feet and a young puppy in his arms.

For the past twenty years, Geoff Billingham has trained more champion Scottish Border Collies than you can shake a crook at. But more than winning, what he really enjoys is teaching a new dog the old tricks.

Geoff's pals twigged him about this. Most Scots have never heard of Dewar's White Label, all of which is exported to the States.

"Hullo, Donald," Geoff took my hand. "How was your trip? You'll be looking for a young bitch, then."

Yes, I was. The trip was okay. Looked like they had plenty of work going on. Hi, Viv.

Geoff smiled ruefully, "Too much if you ask me. Come, I'll show you."

Geoff gestured as we stood on mounds of broken lath and old plaster in the old drover's inn while sheet-rockers' hammers banged away upstairs. The plumbers would be there next week. Painters were expected any day. They'd finished a great green-and-gold sign with a sheepdog rampant, but the ironmonger in Moffat hadn't finished the frame to hang it.

"Geoff," Viv said, "please go in tomorrow and talk to him. He promised it three weeks ago."

Viv Billingham's a vivid woman. She plucks at your sleeve until you see the world she sees: the brilliant dogs, the brilliant hills, the funny tups (rams), the super lambs.

And of course, first thing, I had to inspect their dogs: Garry (retired), Laddie (not working on account of bad feet), Cap, Glen and Holly (mainstays), Lucy (retraining), and Stell and Jed and the pups from two litters. I liked Cap. I thought Holly was wonderful.

After the builders knocked off for the day, we sat in the Billinghams' tiny high-window kitchen and had tea, and cheese on a roll. No, they hadn't heard of any good young bitches for sale.

Geoff couldn't help. Perhaps I'd spot one at the trials. The Neilston Trial was next weekend. "You might look in the paper, Donald. *The Scottish Farmer.* Sometimes it has dogs for sale." I glanced through the current issues but found only a few ads, all for farm dogs. "The good ones are snapped up pretty quickly, I'm afraid," Geoff added.

I looked at my watch. Viv rinsed the teacups at the sink. There was a big pause. Geoff said, "Say, Viv, we haven't been out in weeks. Perhaps we should take Donald to the pub. . . ."

"Just let me feed my dogs and I'll get changed."

The Tweedsmuir Valley is chockablock with sheep-dog lore. James Hogg (Viv's favorite author) shep-herded the Ettrick Valley, on the far side of these hills. Hogg was a fair shepherd but a desperately unsuccess-ful farmer, who (like Bobby Burns) did better writing about farming than practicing it. Hogg started by writ-ing poetry, but Walter Scott convinced him he should turn to prose. Scott gave good advice. James Hogg's poetry is conventional Augustan stuff, neat and dull. His prose is clean as an oiled scythe, affectless, con-temporary. Viv's written two autobiographical books and identifies strongly with Hogg, the shepherd poet of 150 years ago. "You know what they did when James Hogg came to Edinburgh?" she asked angrily. "They made him put on his kilt and dance on the tabletop!"

Downstream, the Tweed passes Easter Dawyck Farm (Johnny Bathgate's great dog Vic), and through the lovely village of Peebles (McTeir's Ben; J. M. Wil-son's Cap, Roy, Glen, Ben). The Crook Inn, where we stopped, was Jock Richardson's local (Wiston Cap, Ri-chardson's Sweep, and Mirk), when he was still shep-herding. When I asked about Jock, Geoff shook his head. Viv said, "Poor Jock. When he was on top, he had no end of friends. Where are they today?"

Shepherds' crooks decorated the pub's walls and dangled from the low beams of the public bar. Half a dozen clunky stools at the corner bar, three tables. We took the table nearest the fire. Geoff and I had a wee dram. Viv liked lemonade in her whisky. A sign on the bar wall defined a "gill" of whisky. Scottish legalese and the pouring gadget on the bottle ensured that you got a gill, not a pennyweight less.

The fireplace was shallow and tall, and welcome heat poured over our legs and shoes. Two years ago, Geoff had been made redundant at the duke of Roxburgh's estate. There are plenty of young men clamoring for a shepherd's place, and very few openings for an older one.

Most Scottish farm lands are owned by great estates: ducal, royal, or commercial syndicates. They lease the hill farms and arable (crop) farms to tenant farmers who have quite a few rights under the law. As long as they aren't harming the property and pay their rents, the tenants cannot be evicted. Their shepherds are lower on the economic scale. Typically, a shepherd gets a salary, a cottage, and some kennel space in an old byre (barn) for his dogs. Sometimes he is allowed to run a few sheep or cows with the farm's own livestock. When a shepherd loses his job, he also loses his home. "We could have gone on the dole," Geoff says sadly, "I suppose we could have moved into council [public] housing. But what would we have done with the dogs?"

There was Holly and Glen, Cap, Garry, and Lucy, Laddie and the puppies: What to do with them all? And giving up the living dogs would be abandoning the others too: Garry's brother Tweed, who was only two years old when he died in Geoff's arms. In the dead of winter, they'd wrapped Tweed in his blue blanket and buried him in the lee of a stone wall. "I think of Tweed now," Viv has written. "Lying in the shadows, his bright eyes like pools of amber light, soul searching, watching the ewes on the hill. . . ."

(33)

The Border Collie and Shepherding Centre was Viv's dream. They'd put on sheepdog demonstrations for coachloads of tourists, explain the shepherd's art, sell Border Collie books and postcards and shepherd's crooks and—this was the good bit—they could keep sheep of their own, breed and train sheepdogs. Viv would have more time to write, and Geoff could do the stick dressing (carving and shaping fancy crooks) he enjoyed.

Above the Tweed was a green schoolhouse they'd refurbish as a shepherding museum and souvenir shop, and across the river—so tiny here it held only salmon fingerlings—was the Billinghams' cottage, a white-washed stable and an ancient stone structure once a drover's inn. The stable would kennel the dogs, and the drover's inn would become a Bed and Breakfast upstairs and, downstairs, a bothy (shepherd's quarters). Viv joked that when Geoff was past it, they'd just sit him in the bothy with a sign round his neck: "SHEPHERD."

Viv obtained a grant from the Scottish Tourist Board and a loan from a temporary bank manager. (When the permanent manager was installed, he told Viv he never would have approved the loan.)

That first winter, their water pump froze, and they had to haul water in buckets to the cottage to wash up and cook and flush the WC. That spring, broke, they rented out their own bedroom to travelers and slept on the livingroom floor.

Tourist coaches stopped that summer to see Viv work her marvelous dogs and maybe buy a book or a couple of postcards. One coach—full of Dutch farmers—ordered lunch in advance, and Viv and Geoff and Geoff, Junior, made a hundred ham sandwiches and had gallons of hot water ready for tea. When the coach arrived, the tourists expected something more, a real sit-down restaurant; so no, they didn't want lunch after all, they'd eat in Moffat. And they wouldn't stop talking while Viv was demonstrating Garry.

"I suppose they were grain farmers," Geoff said. "Not keen on the dogs. It took us weeks to eat those bloody ham sandwiches."

There is nothing snugger than a country pub's fire on a bitter evening, nothing more deceptive.

Viv chattered about Holly, how clever she was, how she'd mother anything: lambs, kittens, ducklings, anything. "God gave me Holly," she said. After a moment Viv grinned like a little girl.

A pair of shepherds at the bar chatted up the barmaid. The fireback was tall and shallow and the heat rolled over us. I hadn't realized how chilled I'd been.

Geoff spoke about Jan, the bitch they'd nicknamed the Bionic Bitch because she could do anything. She could turn on a dime, Jan could, and once won three trials in a single glorious weekend. Dead on the operating table. "That bloody vet," Geoff said. He looked away, stood, asked if I wanted another.

Viv talked about dog honesty, how Garry would never cheat her when he was out of sight, though he might when he was near—just for a joke.

Geoff coughed, set the drinks on the table. "Donald, I'm very much afraid you'd be uncomfortable. We're in a mess. But, if you'd like, you could stay with us."

And Viv added, "That'd be lovely," and I thought so, too. For a second time, in this foreign land, I'd found a home.

That night I slept cramped on the sitting-room couch. The next night I pulled the cushions onto the floor. When the sitting-room fire died after midnight, I drew my coat over the blanket Viv had provided. I had no complaints—this was the warmest room, the only fire in the house. Come morning we'd all gather in the kitchen: sweaters, down vests, for morning tea.

Holly, Laddie, and Garry slept in the kitchen, and,

spotting me for a soft touch, they'd all come over for a pat. I missed my Pip. Holly seemed just the sort of bitch I'd come here for. A smooth-coated two year old, quick but sensible. Strong enough to handle the heavy, bored tups Viv uses for her sheepdog demonstrations, and clever with the stroppy Scottish Blackface ewes who can be very tough protecting their new lambs. When the ewe stamps and threatens, Holly holds her ground, but turns her head, modestly, thus reducing pressure on the ewe. As soon as the ewe relaxes and backs, Holly snaps to and comes on again. It's the same pressure a constable uses on a belligerent drunk. "Would you please get in the car, sir? Yes, sir, in the back."

I can't make an offer for Holly. How can I buy a gift from God? Viv prattles on about fine bitches, splendid bitches: Viv's got fifteen hundred pounds in hand from an American who wants a bitch just like Doug Lamb's Suzy. Viv's gossip is like praising married women to a lonesome bachelor.

The Scottish Borders are the same latitude as Newfoundland, and when we went out I was glad of my long johns and gloves. Geoff wore a torn tweed jacket over his insulated coveralls. Tweedhope is on the brow of a bluff above grazing fields, outlined in broken drystane dykes, cut by the meanderings of the sparkling burns that are here making up the Tweed. I'd follow Geoff on his shepherding rounds. In our green rubber wellies we'd splash through the burns, checking each newborn lamb. Geoff'd pick it up to pat its full belly, "That's all right, old girl, I'll not harm him," and when mother and lamb had got separated (some of the burns were too deep for the lambs to swim), he'd join them back together. Brilliant mosses swirled in the streambeds, oyster catchers and curlews called from the banks. The mists hung above us like theater scrims and the light shimmered. Geoff's young dog, Cap, swirled in and out of the fog. The decision to become a shepherd is an aesthetic decision.

When we went back into the cottage for morning tea, we'd sit across from each other and take our blood-pressure pills, grimacing like kids.

Although Geoff is noted as a dog trainer, in a nation of superb dog men, nothing I see him do, day in and day out, remotely resembles what Americans call "dog training." Training is where you get the dog to do what you want him to, right? When he does wrong you scold him, when he does right you give him a pat or a treat, right? A well-trained dog obeys every command despite his own inclinations, otherwise what's the point?

A couple years ago, a dairyman in Virginia's Shenandoah Valley had a fine young Border Collie, keen as blazes. Since the young dog was often underfoot, the dairyman trained the dog to a "Stay!" so he could go about his chores unhampered. Twice a day he'd send the dog for his cows and after the cows were in the milking parlor he'd point at a patch of cool shade: "Lie down. Stay! You STAY!" One hot August afternoon, the dairyman was working his Holsteins, routine worming, through his cattle chutes. When he shooed his cows out of the pens they came out fast and hard, right over the dog, who never budged from where he'd been told to STAY. The dog was killed, the dairyman was overcome with remorse. He'd never, he vowed, train a dog so well again.

The Scots would say he hadn't trained the dog at all. "The only proper training for a sheepdog is the Hill."

The earliest account of sheepdog training is James Hogg's. His dog Sirrah "was scarcely then a year old, and knew so little of herding, that he had never turned sheep in his life; but as soon as he discovered that it was his duty to do so, and that it obliged me, I can never forget with what anxiety and eagerness he learned his different evolutions. He would try every way deliberately, till he found out what I wanted him to do; and once I made him understand a direction, he never forgot or mistook it again. Well as I knew him, he very often astonished me, for when hard pressed in accomplishing his task, he had expedients of the moment that bespoke a great share of the reasoning faculty."

It is the job of the dog trainer to summon the dog's genetics, not to impose man's will over dog's. It may be worth noting that many Scottish hill dogs *never* know the weight of a collar round their neck.

Sometimes when Geoff goes shepherding, he brings a novice dog along with Cap. The young dog rushes about, trying to understand his life's work and Geoff, without interrupting his tasks, shows it to him. If the dog goes wrong, Geoff tells him. He doesn't pat him or give him treats. "Training unrelated to a sensible way of working sheep makes dogs hot," Geoff says.

Here's a story about Jimmy Wilson and his grand bitch Peg. Peg is getting on now in years, she's nine, but has been on the Scottish team many times. Jimmy shepherds a great hill in the Borders and days go by where he sees more of Peg than his wife. Jimmy is a gentle man but nobody has ever seen him give Peg a pat. Other handlers will pat a dog when they come off the trial field, it's almost custom, but Jimmy never pats Peg. One afternoon, in the beer tent, some of the other Scots were ragging Jimmy about this: and the mild man looked up with a quiet smile, "Why, do you think Peg doesn't know what I think of her?" he asked.

Many Americans confuse training with taking commands. They ask: "How many commands will a Border Collie learn?"

Probably as many as the space shuttle. As many as the United States Marine Corps Drill Team.

When I show Pip off for farm visitors, what they

applaud are his turns and stops. That's because they compare dogs to cars and fear loss of control.

Our American method of pet dog training is designed to be context free: The dog should heel though the skies are bright with Armageddon; the dog should recall though the owner means to have him put down the moment he gets his hands on him. The presumption of this training is that dogs are willful and stupid and, no doubt, some are.

One woman I know, seeing the Border Collie Mike doing stunts in the movie "Down and Out in Beverly Hills" told me, "I could train my dog to do those tricks in two weeks."

Just so. But not on a movie set.

The trainer Tony Illey has said, "The most difficult thing I ever saw a dog do was bring a ewe who'd just lost her lamb through a field full of lambing ewes."

Let me offer a gloss: Ewes with new lambs are extremely protective of their lambs and often charge a dog. When they lose sight of their lamb, they assume the dog has killed it, and despite his teeth will try determinedly to trample him. A ewe who's lost her lamb will rush back and forth seeking it, bleating to other newborn lambs trying to collect one. The other mothers are confused by this, and when the dog gets near them they, too, go on the attack.

Unlike Tony Illey, I don't think what this dog did was difficult. It was impossible. Knowing that the dog can read sheep better than any man and can react much quicker than any man, what commands would you give him?

Correct answer: his name.

The third evening at Tweedhope, out in the fields with Geoff, Cap came over and jumped up for a head scratch. In case I didn't get it (Cap thinks I'm a bit dim), forty minutes later he repeated his greeting. I am quite sure he'll not jump up again, now that he's recognized me as part of his world.

The Billinghams' life had no need for another pair of hands. I cooked a little, washed up, helped Geoff drag lath and broken plaster out of the drover's inn, and when Viv took Holly to London, for an appearance on the BBC's animal program "Caterpillar Trail," I drove them into Edinburgh for the train. Viv was dressed in her TV outfit, quite excited. Holly roamed about Waverly station. When she trotted up to a young couple to say hello, they snubbed her. Brutes.

That evening, after Geoff, Junior, was off to bed, his father and I sat by the fire, talked about men, dogs, landscape, more dogs. Geoff told about a big trial he was winning, last year, until thirteen dogs from the last, a handler keeled over and died. "What had been a very good day became a very bad day," Geoff said. After a moment, he added, "I was very sorry to see him go." After another moment, he said, "He might have waited thirteen more dogs."

I guess I missed my own dogs. I spoke of Pip, all the mistakes I'd made training him. If he hadn't been a better dog than I was a man, I wouldn't be here today. Because of me, he'd never be truly beautiful. I regretted that.

Geoff looked into the fire. Took a sip of whiskey.

"You can't be a dog trainer until you've had regrets. Sometimes I think most of it is regrets." I had to strain to hear Geoff's soft voice. "Jan and that bloody stupid vet. If I hadn't left her with him. I told him what was wrong, you see, and I trusted him. And Tweed, working him so long in the snow. We hadn't been able to get him his vaccination. It was blizzarding, you see, and we couldn't get out." Geoff Billingham sat with his hands in his lap, a gangling aristocrat in a straightback chair, seeing Tweed's amber eyes, the relentless drifting snow. "I sometimes think . . . when I'm on my deathbed . . . they'll come back. All the dogs I've trained will come filing by."

3

The Greatest Sheepdog Handler Since J. M. Wilson

It was one of those rare days when you think you just might get away with it. Spring in the Scottish Lowlands. Along the roadsides, a few brave daffodils were showing their colors and the sun was bright but not warm. In the Highlands, to the north of us, shepherds were still lambing, but that work was finished here, and foolish fat lambs bounced through the fields, baaing after their moms.

The Neilston Sheepdog Trial is the first of the season.

Geoff Billingham was driving. Viv leaned over the front seat, and I sat beside Geoff as navigator. We were lost.

"We should have kept to the motorway," Viv said.

"Donald will guide us," Geoff said, showing a confidence in me thus far unjustified. Geoff Billingham is one of nature's gentlemen.

I said we should turn around. We should have turned at Strathaven. When Geoff stopped the car, the dogs thumped around in the boot, rearranging themselves. "There's no hurry, Geoff," Viv said. "I'm not running Laddie."

Laddie is Garry's son, with the power but not the raw force of his father, and Viv had high hopes for Laddie on the trial field. Laddie did well, too, until he contracted demodectic mange in his feet, and last year, when the poor beast came off the course at the Scottish National, his feet were bloody.

Viv thought he'd heal over the winter and had entered him in the spring trials, but Laddie's feet never got right. Every time tender-footed Laddie needed to cross the gravel path outside the Billinghams' cottage, Viv picked him up and carried him across. Viv is a slight woman. Laddie weighs forty-five pounds.

Once we were back on the proper road, Geoff and Viv speculated happily about friends they might see at this trial, shepherds they hadn't talked to since the International last fall. I asked Geoff if Jock Richardson was likely to be there.

"Well, he does live near," Geoff said. "He's in council housing in Hamilton. But Jock can't drive, you know. They took his license."

All the great sheepdog men, like Jock Richardson, were shepherds or farmers, like John Templeton, who have learned and practiced the shepherd's art.

Sheep rearing in Scotland depends on the habits of sheep. Since this is the reverse of the dominant pattern in American agribusiness, which strains to accommodate animals to the requirements of marketing and machines, this point bears repeating: in Scotland, men adapt themselves to the sheep.

Unless she is physically prevented from doing so, a

ewe will return to the same spot where she was lambed in order to have her own lamb. Since ewes and lambs are left together to graze the high barren hill, they form small groups called hirsels. Think of them as subflocks. A hill may support a thousand ewes, but they'll stay in five or six hirsels, which remain in distinct geographic areas. When gathered into the greater flock for shearing or dipping, the sheep, when released, will sort themselves back into their original hirsels. Think of this as a sheep homing instinct.

So important is this instinct (it has no value in American agribusiness) that Scottish sheep are legally "bound" to the land. If you wish to buy a farm, you must buy the livestock already on it. If you bought a farm and stocked it with strange sheep, your new sheep would drift hither and thither, across the boundary lines, onto the next farm, where they'd mingle with a neighbor's flock and cause no end of difficulties.

More sheep habits: Sheep graze uphill in the evening and downhill in the morning. When startled, they flock together rather than fighting or fleeing individually. They are quite able to distinguish predators and decide which are harmful and which are less so. They rate men and skilled sheepdogs among the less frightening predators, and some dogs have a settling effect on nervous sheep. (An inexperienced sheepdog or feral dog sends sheep into a blind panic.)

In the States, sheep are brought into corrals and chutes for work. In Scotland, except for shearing, dipping, and lamb sales, the sheep stay on the Hill. The shepherd goes to the sheep.

The shepherd strides up the great hill (every morning during lambing) with his crook and his kitbag of necessities (antibiotics and other medicines, perhaps a lamb reviver) dangling from his shoulder. He is accompanied only by his dogs. Among the sheep, indifferent to all but the wildest weather, he must be herdsman, veterinarian, and midwife. On the spot he decides whether a ewe needs help lambing and, if so, performs obstetrics.

When a ewe's lamb dies, the shepherd skins it and attaches the skin over a newborn whose mother can't care for it. Suspiciously, the ewe sniffs the orphan. Smells right? Mine? Finally, the ewe will stand and give the hungry youngster suck.

> There is no good flock without a good shepherd, and there's no good shepherd without a good dog.
>
> —SCOTTISH HOMILY

SHEPHERD SOUGHT ads in *The Scottish Farmer* usually ask for references. They always specify the number of dogs: "Will need own dogs," "Must bring two dogs," and so on.

Without the dogs, high on an unfenced barren hill, no shepherd could do his work. How can a man catch and upend a lambing ewe? How can he drive a hirsel to shelter in the teeth of a storm?

A young part-trained sheepdog can make many mistakes. He can fetch when you want him to drive, nip when he shouldn't, go left when you want him to go right. All these are annoying, but, in time, correctable. The only unforgivable sin in a young sheepdog is deciding to quit and go home. Abandoned by his dog, the shepherd is useless—alone on the high whistling hill, responsible for animals he can neither catch nor gather, sort nor drive.

The sheepdog who abandons his work is lucky to be sold.

At the Neilston Trial, the dogs were the same dogs that yesterday worked ewes with young lambs and would work them again at home this evening. Since new mothers are stroppy and defiant, the dogs were too rough for trial work. The dogs would work too close to the trial sheep and grip too readily because that was the work they were used to.

By summer's end, and the National Trials, these same dogs will have competed in dozens of trials and will be smooth as silk: working well off their nervous charges and reluctant to grip. For shepherds, sheepdog trials are a busman's holiday. For the dogs, they're just another type of work. I hoped that seeing them *now* before some clever handler put a polish on them would compensate for my ignorant eyes. I was seeking a natural dog.

In America, where automobiles conquer undemocratic distances (how can a man be free unless he can drive wherever he wishes, whenever?), the demarcation between rural and urban is indistinct. In Scotland, public transportation and public planning are more powerful than the god-given right of any man to take a beautiful farm and put a McDonald's on it.

Thus Neilston, only fifteen miles from Glasgow Center, is a real farming village, and in the first week of May, every year, Neilston has its agricultural show.

The Neilston Agricultural Society sponsors sheep and cattle competitions and hands out ribbons for the best geese, chickens, rabbits, and ducks. Highland pipers, in full regalia, lead the agricultural parade, and behind them, small children control their ponies with just a little help from Da. The Methodist Church ladies have their annual book fair in one tent; there's a tearoom in another. There are a thousand people here today. It's May and pale-skinned youths have their shirts off to get some sun.

This was the sort of day that meant trouble for me when I was growing up in Montana. We'd find someone old enough to buy cases of beer, borrow a car, and drive into the spring countryside. By nightfall, we'd be drunk and sick and the light would have collapsed, but that day, ah that day!

Neilston's beer tent is next to the trial field, and the loo's just behind. The men's loo is a blue plastic tarpaulin stretched around uprights to form a ten-foot grassy square where men can pee. There's one Porta-John for a waiting line of women.

Neilston is the first trial of the season that will culminate, in September, at the International (this year at Blair Atholl, Perthshire). Trial men have come here today to work the kinks out of trusted older dogs or to get younger ones started.

The trial secretary is a portly red-faced young man. Yes, Jock Richardson is here. "I didn't know him. He came to me and asked if he could still make his entry, and I said what's your name? 'Richardson,' he said. 'First name?' And he said, 'Jock.' Wasn't I embarrassed?"

Though Neilston is a short awkward course, there are brilliant handlers here today. Both John Templeton and David McTeir have won the International. Alasdair MacRae took the Scottish National in 1986; others are regulars on the Scottish team.

But most of the shepherds here today are retired, elderly men who sold their dogs when they came off the Hill and, perhaps, weren't such keen trialists in their youth. Neilston is the first Scotrail stop out of Glasgow, and it's a braw day to get out of the city, greet old friends, admire the bonny young dogs making their try. These retired men are dressed in their best suits, three-piece tweeds. Many wear the ISDS badge in their lapels. (The dog silhouetted on this badge is Wiston Cap.) Each shepherd carries his crook—a briar staff surmounted by a carved sheep's horn handle. They made their crooks themselves, between chores, when they were lads on the Hill. "How are you keeping? Have you wintered well?"

I was keen to meet Jock Richardson. I'd heard rumors that a head injury had reduced him. I knew he rarely trialed and no longer did well at it. But he had been brilliant with the dogs and a wonderful athlete, and I'd be honored to shake his hand.

You cannot talk about Jock Richardson without, in the same breath, talking about Wiston Cap.

Cap, who died in 1979, still haunts the memories of those shepherds who saw him. He was stylish, good natured ("If he was a man he would have come right up to you and stuck out his hand and said, 'How do you do'; that's how Cap was"), a splendid hill dog.

Detractors say Cap was weak. At the Cardiff International, in 1965, the trial that made Cap's reputation, Cap took ten long, long minutes to get his sheep into the pen. Ninety seconds is more usual. But Cap's sons and grandsons have won six Internationals.

Viv Billingham says, "Wiston Cap just seemed to float over the ground."

In his trialing career, Wiston Cap only won five big trials, but sheepdog trialing is a three-species sport, full of chance. If man and dog are unlucky, they may draw sheep with a ewe used to going her own way, a worm-ridden ewe, one sickly, and balky. Many trials are decided by narrow margins, and the sheep are accomplices in the score. When Jock Richardson ran Cap, handlers thought Cap was the best dog in Britain. When he lost a trial, they said Cap just wasn't the best dog on that day.

In his pedigree, Wiston Cap had sixteen crosses back to J. M. Wilson's great wartime dog, another Cap (#3036 in the ISDS registry). From 1939 to 1945, the ISDS suspended trialing, so Wilson's Cap never had a chance to run in the International, but shepherds who saw him admired him, and he was widely used as a stud dog. He sired 118 daughters.

For forty years, until his death in 1975, J. M. Wilson was an overpowering figure in sheepdog trialing. He won nine International Sheepdog Trials, and dogs he trained won two more. No other man has ever won more than three Internationals. (J. M. retired three of the huge silver-studded International shields and donated them to small Highland trials, where they're awarded to this day.) Scots, usually chary with praise, recall J. M. as "The Great" J. M. Wilson.

A shepherd's son, J. M. could, by the age of twelve, ken each of his father's thousand ewes as he passed through them on his way to school. "Ken" in this instance means he knew each ewe's history, health problems, and where and how she'd lamb. Before he got his first dog, his father used J. M. and his brother Ben to do the dogs' work, hieing after wild Highland sheep on the steep crags and hills. J. M. became a tenant farmer, and an increasingly prosperous sheep breeder; he was still a young man when he bought Whitehope Farm near Innerleithin.

Not every hill in the Scottish Borders is hard; some of the eastern and southern slopes are protected, more fortunate. Beautiful Whitehope Farm is a thousand feet above sea level, and the Hill behind it that encloses the steading is just twice that.

From the 1930s on, J. M. Wilson was a favorite interview subject for *The Field* and *The Scottish Farmer*. Although different photographers were assigned to the stories, each took the same three pictures. Wilson himself: The photos showed a young man who liked a joke and an older man who liked a sardonic joke. Then there'd be a picture of one of Wilson's famous dogs: Cap, or Moss, or Bill, or Bill II, or Corrie, or one-eyed Roy, the only dog who ever won the International three times. So many dogs. Finally, there'd be the big photograph of Whitehope, taken each time from the identical vantage point, at the base of the softly sweeping Hill, across the crystal-clear stream—Leithien Water.

Wilson, the most brilliant sheepdog man of his time, was also the most prominent Scottish Blackface breeder. Year after year, Whitehope tups set records at the Lanark tup sales. When sheep are bound to a farm, the only practical way to improve a flock is by importing high-grade tups, and Whitehope tups were so sought after that the *averages* for Wilson's consignments were double and sometimes triple his nearest competitor.

Farmers who daren't even bid on Wilson's best tup *would* bid on his lesser animals. "Oh aye," they'd say, leaning over the dyke with their neighbor, "yon tup of mine came from Whitehope—the place that had the record-breaking tup at Lanark. Thirty-five hundred for a tup, what's the world coming to?" This canny farmer only paid a thousand for *his* Whitehope tup. Quite a bargain, yes?

In the thirties, sheepdog trialing was viewed as a crude sport, with all the social cachet of, say, coon-dog trialing in the States. Although the ISDS Secretary always dug up minor royals to award prizes at those early Internationals, press coverage ignored sheepdogs and shepherds in favor of gossip about the royal party and photos of prominent country gents mingling with their social inferiors. The country gents often brought their pet dogs to the International. Fancy dogs: poodles, Great Danes, Bouviers des Flandres.

There's a wonderful photograph of J. M. Wilson accepting the trophy he'd won with Fly (1928). The gaily dressed marchioness who presented him the prize requested that he sing a couple verses of a "darkie" song before she gave him his award. So, after breeding, training, polishing, and running a world-class athlete in the most difficult test of man and dog ever devised, J. M. Wilson sang a few choruses of "Oh Dem Gals" before they gave him his trophy.

J. M.'s old pal, Johnny Bathgate, says, "J. M. was a longheaded chap."

He was also unsentimental, a man who didn't suffer fools gladly. One woman handler came to J. M. for advice about her dog who wouldn't take his left flanks no matter how she begged and pleaded.

"Put a bit of lead in his left lug (ear)," Wilson advised.

"Oh. But how would I do that?"

"Madam, with a gun."

Good dog men are frequently asked questions that are beneath them, questions to which there are no proper answers except, perhaps, "If you could understand the answer, you wouldn't be asking the question."

In the States, a disproportionate number of good sheepdog handlers were skilled horsemen before they turned to the dogs. It was Vicki Hearne who explained this to me. "You can't be as stupid with a horse as a dog," she laughed. "Horses are too big."

Many other top dog men were athletes before they got involved with dog athletes. Competitiveness, I thought. They do so well because they are accustomed to competition. But mine was a shallow answer. If raw competitiveness was the key, our trial fields would be cluttered by arbitrageurs and property developers and movie producers and other inflamed ego types. I think sheepdog trialing is safe from Donald Trump.

It is obvious, at a sheepdog trial, that the dog does most of the work. It is, after all, a *dog* trial. But top dog men have the lightness, grace, and precision of great athletes. If a klutz did manage to get hold of a great trial dog, a Wiston Cap, the klutz wouldn't start winning sheepdog trials—unless the man was clever enough to let the dog school *him*.

In 1987, at the Blue Ridge Trial, the lot where the sheep went after their run was too near the course. The sheep had run the day before and knew that lot promised rest and shade.

You may recall that the Blue Ridge is run in a great grassy bowl with the handler standing on one rim. When the dog brought the sheep around the man and started them on their drive away, the sheep tended to drift downhill, toward the bowl bottom, until, fifty yards along, the sheep would remember that blessed lot, over the rim on the right and they'd bolt for it, pellmell. To keep them on line, the dog would be on their left and when they shot off to the right, he was in the worst position to prevent their escape. Bill Berhow, one of America's best young dog men, watched as handler after handler took DQ ("off-course") for their score. Bill had three apparent choices, none attractive. (1) Let the sheep drift going down into the bowl, hold his Nick dog at their heels and prevent their sudden bolt. Possible points off for drifting: 3–8? (2) Bill could wait until the sheep bolted and cry Nick around from left to right—but that stunt wasn't working for anyone. No dog was quick enough to catch them on the course. (3) When they broke, Bill could send Nick directly to their heads, around the left. Heading the sheep was a slight fault, 1–2 points off. Most of the better handlers adopted this strategy.

Bill and Nick had a nice outrun, nice lift, and the sheep came up to the post slowly, around his legs, and Bill sent Nick to the left to hold them on line, perfect, perfect, and then, Bill cried Nick around to the right, *before* the sheep decided to bolt and when they did, Nick was right there to hold them. A perfect save, and Bill Berhow and Nick won the Blue Ridge that year by one point. When I asked Bill how he knew when to send Nick he said, "I could see that lead ewe was thinking about taking off."

Any athlete, dog or man, must master the flowing gestalt of things, must comprehend *physical* meaning, must be slightly ahead of the action. Amateurs think of a sheepdog trial as static geometry: a pattern of invisible straight lines the sheep must traverse. That's mistaking the choreography for the ballet.

Often I've watched the beginners bring their dogs to sheep for the first time, and from the way the men walked, how they held their stiff bodies, I knew it was hopeless. You cannot train a dog if you're bumping into things all the time.

Nor can you train a sheepdog if you have too great faith in words. The mental model for too many would-be dog trainers is the drill sergeant: "Right About Face!, Left Shoulder Harms!" And dogs *can* be trained to those useless mechanical perfections. After all, that dairy farmer's dog did STAY, even when it killed him.

But such dogs are no good on the trial field, no good on the Hill.

The most important command any dog has is his name. "Pip" means, "Off!" "Pay attention!" "Think!" "Get up!" "Come here!" and, half a dozen other things depending on how and when it's uttered. His name is the first word any dog learns yet, sometimes, when a sheepdog is sold, the new trainer will change the dog's name. It is common for a new trainer to change all the dog's whistle commands and sometimes reverse his flanks so "Away to me" no longer means "Go right" but now means "Go left." In a skilled trainer's hands, the dog's confusion is brief.

One time Jack Knox was working a student's dog in a five-acre pasture. When you're "putting the flanks" on a dog, you wait until the dog wants very much to go left, is actually started left, and then command him to the opposite side. Since your new command violates the dog's previous training, his own developed sense of where to be, his balance, you announce to the dog that a new level of understanding is required.

This young dog went out, out, started to head its sheep, swung around to the left, Jack whistled "Go right," and the dog instantly took the command. When the dog had found a new balance point, Jack whistled the dog "Down." There is nothing particularly remarkable about this except one thing: This dog had *never* been trained to whistles.

When Jack, or any other top dog trainer goes out with his dog, he becomes pure communication. The trainer's body and voice are the command.

That this communication works for dogs who never take their attention off their sheep, rarely *look* at the man and, over great distances, cannot possibly see him, extends the boundaries of communication or perhaps affirms the primacy of intention over fact.

Much of J. M. Wilson's dog history occurred before the distemper vaccine, and his kennels were hit hard by the disease. Roy, thrice winner of the International, barely survived a bout, and many other fine dogs died. In 1935 Wilson was working a young part-trained dog on the Hill when the dog had a sudden fit and attacked him. Wilson tried to toss his coat over the dog to subdue it, but the dog savaged his hand and wrist until J. M. shot it. Wilson took blood poisoning and very nearly died. His was an excruciatingly painful wound. But when a reporter from the *Scottish Farmer* visited him in the hospital, "Wilson lay back on his pillow, his heavily bandaged hand outstretched before him. 'It was the most promising dog I ever had,' he said softly. 'The famous Craig was its father and his son was the double of him. He had the same markings, the same nature, the same tricks. . . .'"

Maybe Geoff Billingham is right. All dog training is regrets.

Wilson and his wife had no children, but J. M. had protégés. Dougie Lamb remembers being in the beer tent midway through a National trial when J. M. came bursting in. Everybody set down their drams. In his powerful voice, J. M. said, "When I was young, I'd watch Sandy Milar because I could learn from him. Out there is a man you can learn from."

That man was Jock Richardson, who was as gifted with dogs as J. M. was and, perhaps, a bit kinder. Jock wasn't longheaded at all.

Jock Richardson grew up a poor city boy and came

to livestock work after he was full grown. Before he took his first shepherding job, he trekked around the countryside with a stallion, offering him at stud. When Jock became a shepherd at Lynne, near Peebles, David McTeir worked nearby at Milton Manor and Johnny Bathgate tenanted Easter Dwyck. The three friends traveled to the sheepdog trials together. Up at Saturday dawn to do chores before they set out, they wouldn't be home again until dark. On the return trip, Johnny Bathgate'd get sleepy and curl up against the door, and David McTeir'd drive and Jock Richardson would ride in the back seat with the dogs, singing.

J. M. Wilson took an interest in Jock Richardson and gave him young dogs to train. When the young shepherd qualified Wiston Cap to run at the Cardiff International, J. M. took Jock under his wing. Now, J. M. was no drinking man. Jock Richardson was so nervous that day at Cardiff, he drank four bottles of (nonalcoholic) ginger beer.

Wiston Cap was a hearty black-and-white dog with considerable white on his face and big upstanding lugs—like his wartime ancestor Wilson's Cap #3036. Wiston Cap was twenty-one months old when he ran the International, and when he won it, it was about the same thing as a high school boy quarterbacking the American Super Bowl. Border Collies are a slow-maturing dogs. Dogs run in *nursery* trials until they're 2½. The International is a desperately difficult, big, big course. The outrun is half a mile, and dogs frequently work at twice that distance from their handlers. Experienced, steady trial dogs fail to finish the course more often than not, and many fine young dogs lose it altogether.

But what young Wiston Cap did at that daunting trial was win it, and when Jock and Cap came off the course, J. M. came up to Jock, grinning. "Your dog could do that course again," he said.

Wiston Cap became the most sought-after stud dog in Border Collie history, and soon Jock Richardson was pocketing better than a thousand pounds a year in stud fees (shepherd's wages at the time being forty pounds a week).

Jock got Mirk and Sweep out of Cap, and when the great dog's sons started to win trials, Jock Richardson was a rich man—in his kennels he had the three best sheepdogs in Great Britain.

Wiston Cap provoked deep goofiness among breeders. The man who bred Cap repeated the exact mating over and over, hoping to get another Cap. (Geoff Billingham had one of these pups, a bonny big thing named Wattie Cap, who died of pneumonia.) An English solicitor deliberately bred Wiston Cap's sons to Cap's daughters until he created a pup with "86% Wiston Cap Blood." The pup did look like the old man, but, of course, he never amounted to much, and I shudder to think how many deformed pups were produced by those matings.

And Jock was a splendid handler. Hamish MacLean remembers a trial where the pen was built so narrow nobody could get the skittish ewes inside. Jock, working with Sweep that day, put the ewes into single file and they followed the leader in, quite docily. (Under pressure, sheep do not *go* in single file.) Then, hurrying, Jock pressed the sheep against the judge's car to get a quick shed.

But that's not the picture that stays in Hamish MacLean's mind. It's afterward, after the applause stopped and Jock took his sheep off the course. Then, his sheep put away, out of sight of the spectators, Jock walked alone with his great dog and Sweep jumped up, again and again, his head as high as Jock's own.

Johnny Bathgate and David McTeir stopped traveling to trials with Jock. I asked Johnny why.

"Because he would nae come home," Johnny said.

* * *

The handlers at Neilston crowd around Jock Richardson and shake his hand. "Have you wintered well?"

Dougie Lamb is a prosperous, well-regarded man in his forties, but he's awkward as a boy introducing me to Jock Richardson, who ran his famous dogs twenty years ago.

"Jock's the greatest sheepdog handler since J. M. Wilson," Dougie states, and doesn't know what to say after he's said it.

Jock Richardson's a big man with smile lines at the corners of his eyes. He's got the swollen fingers of a man who's done a lifetime of manual work, and his left hand is wrapped in a handkerchief. He caught his hand in the car door, he says and the men who surround him are all hoping that's how it really happened, that he was sober. Jock's dressed swell in a gray pinstripe suit, striped blue shirt, and purple tie.

Dougie points to Jock's crook, which has "J. Richardson" carved in the handle. "Oh, that'll be worth a fortune one day."

There's a young ratty-looking dog at Jock's heel. Nothing connects them but the bit of twine between his collar and Jock's hand. Nothing.

Dougie says, "Oh, when Jock was on the Hill and the heather so thick, and the Americans came over, Cap'd go up and they'd see a thing or two."

Jock's new dog is named Cap, too. Yes, he's one of Wiston Cap's grandsons. Yes, he's just like Wiston Cap except smaller. A bit smaller. Jock doesn't expect to win. He borrowed the dog this morning from his son-in-law's farm.

"Will you have a wee dram, then, Jock?"

"Nae. Not 'til I've had my run."

I ask him about Wiston Cap, and he tells how Cap used to come into the kitchen and lay his head on his shoes. Jock's told this story so many times the life has drained out of what was once a true thing.

(56)

Now, Jock works part-time for a dairy farmer. The farmer drove him here today.

When it came my turn to buy a round, I passed right by Jock Richardson without asking what he wanted, but when I started for the tent, courteous Geoff asked Jock and, yes, Jock would have a half pint of bitter.

Later I was to argue with Viv and Geoff. "If somebody has a drinking problem and says he doesn't want a drink, it's wrong to press one on him."

Geoff thought that was treating Jock like a child. "It's for Jock to say 'nae,' " he said.

A month after Neilston, I spoke with a man who'd been on the Scottish team with Jock the year he qualified Sweep to run in the International. The night before the Championship, Jock's teammate paused at the door to Jock's hotel room, which was "full of those Welsh cronies of his, and everybody drinking and having a grand time and Jock was wrestling Sweep, just rolling that big dog around on the floor. Of course, next morning, when Jock and Sweep went out on the course, oh, Jock was no bloody use at all."

When he was in the money, sometimes Jock wouldn't return from a Saturday trial until Tuesday. He'd stop at each pub along the way, and Cap'd be wandering around outside. And there's more than one sly Scottish farmer who used that great dog to line his bitch while Jock was inside, too drunk to know.

After a shoving match in the beer tent at one Scottish National, the ISDS suspended Jock.

J. M. Wilson washed his hands of Jock, and John Angus MacLeod got his start when J. M. lent him seventy-five pounds to buy Glen away from Jock. (John Angus went to the International with Glen.)

It was the waste that offended prudent Scottish sensibilities. All that money. Those grand dogs. While he was suspended, Jock couldn't register pups with the ISDS, so he sold Mirk and Sweep to a Welsh pal of his, a livestock dealer. Some say it wasn't a real sale. Some say Jock was still getting the stud fees as the Welsh man bred those two great dogs until they were so frail they had to be lifted onto their bitches.

Today, at Neilston, Jock walks to the post with a jaunty young man's stride and stands at the post like he owns the place, the ratty looking Cap dog at his side. His commands are very quiet as Cap negotiates the course, and Cap has a fair run going until, on the drive, Jock gives Cap the wrong command.

Dougie Lamb groans aloud. "Jock's reflexes are gone, you see. That's not too bad a dog."

Jock's mistake has cost him enough points that he'll be out of the prize list. With a boyish grin, he turns to the judge. "Disqualified," he says, and walks off the course.

Watching Jock Richardson past his prime was like catching the faintest waft of a beautiful woman's lingering scent after she's left the room.

In the beer tent, I meet Jock's employer, who is a corpulent man, perfectly satisfied with himself. He jabs his finger toward Jock. "He used to be a champion at this, you know. Oh yes, very famous."

It was March of 1979, a bitter March in the Lammermuir hills, and Old Wiston Cap was fifteen. Jock had been to the pub that night and was dressed in his best slacks and sport coat, but stopped to check his dogs before he came into the cottage to bed.

There was snow on his coat and cap when he came inside and said softly to his wife, "Mary, Cap's dying."

Jock went back outside then. His good wife waited for him to come in as the fire grew ashy white and cold. Mary went to bed, and it was a chill bed that night, a lonely one.

In the light of dawn, Mary Richardson, frightened now, stepped outside the cottage door and hurried to the row of doghouses in the steading. Jock Richardson sat, snowy and coatless beside the body of his great dog. No telling how long he'd sat there. He'd wrapped Cap in his only sport coat to keep the old boy warm.

I have always wanted to know what a man like that might say to a dog like that on his death night. When I spoke to Jock Richardson, of course, I had no right to ask.

At the Neilston trial, neither Viv nor Geoff did very well. Geoff retired Cap, and Holly rushed her work and came fourth. Dougie Lamb and Suzie were second, and Alasdair MacRae was third with his black unregistered bitch, Bute. Alasdair seemed surprised when I asked if I could stop by. "Oh, I suppose you could. . . ." John Templeton won the trial with his eminent Roy.

I go into the loo for a quick pee and the ground is squoogy under my feet and the old man hunched on his side on the grass has pissed himself. The ruddy young trial secretary and I lift him out of the muck to a place where he can sit, and the young man asks, "Where do you bide, sir? If you'll tell me where, I'll see you home."

The old man's cap lies wet in his lap. His three-piece suit was fresh from the dry cleaners only this morning.

"Please, sir. Glasgow Central, please sir."

"What can this American be thinking of us?" the young man says. "Where do you want to go?"

"Glasgow Central, please sir."

"Do you have a ticket? Shall I put you on the train?"

"Please, sir."

Dusk is long in the springtime, so far north and it doesn't go completely dark until ten. On the way back to Tweedhope, we get right on the motorway, no problem. Geoff is upset about Jock. "Do you know what he's doing? Jock told me he's digging ditches for that dairy man. Digging ditches, a man like him."

We turn off the motorway north of Moffat and get on the back road.

As the car soars up, up, into the hill, Viv puts a tape on. It's an ancient frail song and she sings along:

"Oh, the wild mountain thyme, grows around the purple heather . . . Will you go, Laddy, will you go? . . ."

Geoff says, "The lads used to follow Jock Richardson. It was like he was the pied piper. At one trial, Jock came out of the beer tent and found a gang of boys, wrestling. 'No, no,' says Jock. 'You'll have to do that properly.'

"And he created this contest, you know, eliminations and all that. There was to be a prize for the winning lad, fifty pence.

"Jock was judge and he declared the winner of each elimination match until finally, there were only two lads left, a big lad and a wee lad, much younger. Oh, that wee lad, he was giving it all he had. And he was having the better of the other lad, too. The wee lad's sister came along then and says, 'Mum wants you. Right now.'

"So the lad looked up at Jock, and Jock jerked his thumb. 'Get along now,' Jock says, 'Your mother wants you.'

"So the lad gets up and dusts himself off. Oh, he was heartbroken but not going to show it, mind. And the lad got, oh, twenty feet away before Jock called him, "Laddie,' and Jock went into his pocket and gave him the fifty p first prize.

"That's how Jock was. And the thing is, that day, I happen to know, that fifty p was all the money Jock Richardson had."

4

The Man Who'd Sell His Shoes

He was a gash an faithfu tyke,
As ever lap a sleugh or dyke.
His honest, sonsie, bawsnt face
Ay gat him friends in ilka place;
His breast was white, his tousie back
Weel clad wi coat o glossy black;
His gawsie tail, wi upward curl,
Hung owre his hurdies wi a swirl.

—ROBERT BURNS,
"THE TWA DOGS"

Every single thing I've learnt about sheepdogs has come hard for me. I'd expected lessons in Scotland but not these lessons. I'd come to buy a bitch. What, besides money, was required of me?

I don't know how I'd imagined it: Perhaps I'd hoped some American-speaking Scottish dog dealer would trot out a half-dozen fine young bitches, one on the heels of another, each properly bred and trained, each with a price tag coyly peeping from her feminine collar.

Two of Viv's bitches, Stel and Lucy, might be for sale, though never a direct word was said about it. True, Stel and Lucy *were* shown in their best light, but

The Best Light is the only illumination Viv Billingham has. Stel was a shy bitch, and when last I tried to train a shy bitch, she ran from me to the top of the barnyard hill and wouldn't come until I went indoors and my wife called her. Lucy had been trained by an obedience handler and now, working sheep, she was awfully unsure of herself, constantly looking back to her handler for reassurance.

Once, in passing, Viv said a certain Scot would give two thousand pounds for Holly if Viv was willing to sell. I couldn't afford this clever, young, beautiful bitch if she *had* been for sale. I could, however, yearn like a schoolboy. I must have taken fifty photographs of Holly. Viv asked if I'd send her one.

"Sure."

Monday morning, after Neilston, Geoff mentioned that other guests were expected at Tweedhope and it wasn't until I had my car packed that I realized I'd been asked to leave, so gently was it done.

Butte, Montana, where I was born, is in the Rocky Mountains, and like all mountaineers, I'm an altitude snob. I never expected the Scottish Highlands to be *high*, but they rose beside the road like leviathans: sheer, heads lost in the mists, their northern flanks slathered with snow. Snow in the second week of May. Christ!

There were no fences across desolate Rannoch Moor. Sheep grazed near the road, untended, and here and there, a heap of wooly scraps in the ditch marked where a car had killed one. On the left, the knife ridges of the White Corries. J. M. Wilson had a dog he called "Corrie."

The road dropped into Glencoe, curving into the broad, haunted glen where the last highlanders to submit to King William were assaulted in their sleep, pursued by bloody knives through the winter snows. It may be that William never read the order he signed "to extirpate that sect of thieves." He may have been as blood innocent as he claimed.

It wasn't the Glencoe murders, qua murders, that shocked the Scottish conscience. The MacDonalds of Glencoe were a rough bunch of cattle thieves, and murders weren't uncommon in the eighteenth century. What stirred up the highlanders' wrath was the abuse of hospitality: The MacDonalds were slain by their *guests*. Scots did the deed willingly. I did not know whether my kinfolk were with them, but they easily might have been.

It was quite cold. Despite the clear sky, winter hadn't withdrawn far from the Highlands.

Beyond Glencoe, beyond Fort William, established, as Sam Johnson said, to subdue, "savage clans and raving barbarians," road signs were printed in Gaelic as well as English. So early in the spring, the brightest color was the gorse, vulgar metallic orange bushes splotching the shoreline of the steel gray lochs. Occasional cottages were always white and lonely, tucked beneath the stark hills for comfort.

Glenfinnan meant nothing to me. Charlie *who?* Glenfinnan was a loch between two farms with sheepdogs. I got out of the car and stretched.

In 1745, Bonnie Prince Charlie sailed from France with a force of seven men and vague promises of French assistance. When Charlie landed, the highlanders were appalled. Where was Charlie's army? Many of the highlanders were Jacobites—adherents to the Jamesian line of Scottish kings—and Charlie was the rightful heir. Many highlanders were, like Charlie, Catholics. Dramatically, Charlie ordered his French ship to abandon him on the beach. He may have been feckless, but he was no coward. He shamed the highlanders into joining him, and here, on the shores of Loch Glenfinnan, from dawn to dusk one grand day, the Highland clans pledged Charlie fealty.

They weren't *just* romantics. Since the union of the Scottish and English parliaments in 1707, Scotland had been depressed, and doubtless the clansmen were hungry. Doubtless, some slipped out of their remote glens to join Charlie for the pure unadulterated hell of it. After the Rebellion collapsed, Donald (a highlander), was asked if he'd really thought the Jacobites could prevail. "I ne'er thocht aboot it," he said, "I just thocht hee pleasant it wad be to see Donald riflin' London."

On this May morning, two tourist coaches were parked here. A tour guide had a smoke. Casually dressed tourists took snapshots. Kids ran for the loo. A statue of a stern highlander stared out at the loch as if Charlie might yet reappear.

From Glenfinnan, Charlie's army marched on Edinburgh (which fell to them with glad hosannas). They licked the English at Preston Pans. They turned south toward London. Oh, it was a stirring sight.

Beyond Loch Glenfinnan is empty country until the sea. Great sea lochs stretch out, promising all the freedom of the western oceans. The caravan parks were empty this early in the season. Rafts of salmon cages floated in the lochs, and twice I saw helicopters ferrying salmon from freshwater to saltwater lochs; precisely transported as their luminous bodies underwent the miraculous sea change.

I hadn't expected Scotland to disturb me. I'd come here to buy a dog.

The Scottish farmer is hemmed in by regulations that Americans would find intolerable. The Scot can't tear down old buildings or erect new ones without permission. He can't plow down an ancient hedgerow or flatten a dyke. British government inspectors tell the farmer how often to dip his sheep, and they verify that his beasts are treated humanely.

In exchange, the farmer is protected from rapacious development and devastating market shifts. He's paid a subsidy for each productive ewe, government agencies handle his wool and ensure a market for his lambs. Scottish farmers aren't as desperate as farmers in the States.

Still, like his American counterpart, the Scot is feeling a squeeze. At one time, a shepherd would look after seven hundred ewes, but nowadays twice that number is more common, and some farmers quit employing shepherds altogether, relying on contract shepherds for the lambing, shearing, and dipping.

Alasdair MacRae is a contract shepherd in Kinlochmoidart. In 1985, a young man, he won the Scottish National Sheepdog Trial. He went to Holland for a couple of years, putting on sheepdog demonstrations in a theme park. On his return to Scotland, his pals asked him, "How was it, Alasdair? How about the Dutch lassies?"

"Big," he said. "Aye, they are big."

At Neilston, Saturday, he'd run his dog, Star, and his three-year-old unregistered bitch, Bute. Bute is a medium-size black bitch, a strong bitch. Since unregistered dogs can't compete in the National, Alasdair would have to get Bute registered on merit, an aggravating expensive process. That's why I hoped Bute might be for sale.

Alasdair's cottage was a midsize stone Victorian farmhouse with its front door opening on the narrow Kinlochmoidart road. "Hello, Mrs. MacRae, is your husband home?"

The homely girl in the thick yellow fish-smelling coveralls tugged at her hair and laughed nervously, "Oh, I'm not Mrs. MacRae. He should be home soon. I'm up from London. I just board with Alasdair."

She worked at the salmon fishery. I asked her how she liked it, after London, so deep in the highlands.

"At least you can walk down the street at night," she said.

Along the single track road outside, for miles, I hadn't seen another car.

Alasdair MacRae is a stocky man in his twenties with a presence that makes him seem taller than he is. He's unshaven, wears a T-shirt with a SURFER legend. "Would you like tea, Donald? I think there's beer my brother's brought, but it'll be warm."

The farmhouse kitchen is bare and low ceilinged, the light filtering through the windows seems gray-green. Alasdair doesn't know why I've come and never stays still. He asks me, right off, if I know a dog called Mirk. An American dog buyer had Mirk off Alan Gordon. Mirk went over three years past.

"There are a lot of Mirks in America."

"Aye. Right you are." Alasdair clasped his hands together. "We'll have to drive a bit to where I can work the dogs."

A mile below Alasdair's cottage, we abandoned the paved road for a rough track, forded a burn, passed into a skinny valley with steep crags on either side. It was the kind of place where western movies used to stage their Indian ambushes.

Alasdair pointed. I shaded my eyes, and way up there, I spotted the sheep: two or three, no, more like a dozen—another lot in that ravine there. I couldn't tell how many, they were too far.

When Alasdair sent Bute, she shot down the valley until she hit a rockfall to clamber up and lunged up the rocks. She disappeared behind a rocky knob. If I had asked Pip to get up that slope, the climb would have killed him.

Once Bute is out of sight, we stand about, take a leisurely pee, and it's more minutes before we see Bute, fifteen hundred feet up, a dot on the skyline behind the highest sheep. She descends and disappears again.

If she makes a mistake, the sheep will bolt off the precipice, and most will be dead by the time they quit rolling. A dog wouldn't survive a fall either. If these were my animals, I'd be sweating, but Alasdair seems oblivious to the risk. As he speaks, the Scot takes in gasps of air, like an opera singer. "They're down in that dip there" (gasp). "Aye. It's quite steep, really." He whistles (gasp). "The sheep are usually gathered along there. We bring them into the fold at the far end, there." Whistles again. "That's what Bute's thinking I'm asking her to do" (gasp). (It was only later, after I heard other Scots punctuating their sentences with quick intakes of air, that I realized his is a dialect pattern, not emphysema.)

Bute finds a relatively mild decline and five minutes later the ewes arrive, panting, at Alasdair's feet.

I am dazzled, can't trust myself to speak, "Jesus, what a dog."

Blandly chipper. "Aye. She's quite a useful beast."

In the guest room back at the cottage, there is a stack of mattresses beside my bed. "My brother, Farquar, will stop by late, or some of his friends." Alasdair grins. "Sometimes I don't know who's here until they come down in the morning."

While Alasdair washes up before dinner, I sneak out to the ratty kennels behind the house. Bute is uneasy at my inspection but stands it long enough for me to see she's got dark, hard eyes. She's a more businesslike, less affectionate bitch than Viv's Holly.

We took Alasdair's car to the restaurant. The countryside here is silver lochs and glistening tidal flats, and tidal islands covered with shoulder high brush. The road winds down the coast and Alasdair drives like a young man who knows just exactly where he's going. We dip down beside a skinny mud flat, "In summer, picnickers try to cross that and then the tide comes in," he snorts.

He gestures at a brushy island, and smiles a strange smile. "Have you met John Angus MacLeod? No, he wasn't at Dalrymple, I've no doubt John is lambing yet. He comes from over there."

Alasdair's a man with opinions. Nursery trials (where the youngest dogs compete): "They were all right at first until they started awarding trophies at the end of the season. Now they push the dogs to get them ready for the nurseries; they push them to get them ready for the open trials. They ruin young dogs."

And prices, he says, are mad: "Fifteen hundred pounds for a dog that throws its tail about. A thousand pounds for a dog with a savage grip. Now, that black Bute bitch, she's worth, realistically, eight hundred pounds."

Casually I asked him, "What are her faults?"

Alasdair shot me a hard look and didn't reply right away. "I don't care to talk about my dogs' faults," he said. After a couple miles he squeezed out, "Bute doesn't care for the shedding, but she's getting better at it."

The restaurant was in a hotel where Alasdair often played with a traditional Highland band on Saturday nights. A plain room with sturdy tables and white paper tablecloths. Alasdair ordered a double orange juice in a pint glass please, and I wanted a bitter. Leaning across the table, I asked if the black bitch was for sale.

"Nae. I haven't time or petrol to drive across the country looking for another." The young shepherd warns me, in detail, that any good handler can conceal the faults of a dog (at least from inept American eyes).

We order salmon, another bitter, another double OJ. Alasdair is going on about devious handlers, but I am working up my nerve and everything he says is white noise. I warmed to Viv's Holly more than Bute, but the hard unregistered bitch may well be a better dog. She may be too much for me to handle. "I'll give you twelve hundred pounds for Bute," I manage to choke it out. I drain my bitter.

Alasdair is annoyed. Says he's flattered and not that he can't use the money but no. "Far too many good dogs are sold to the States. It's ridiculous. Did you know we're importing Aberdeen Angus cattle from

Canada? From Canada, mind. It's just to get the blood-lines back. But once a dog is gone, it's gone."

He names several good dogs that shouldn't have gone. He says, "That Glen dog Johnny Templeton sold to the States was much better than the dog Johnny kept. It's ridiculous."

I felt like a Quaker slave trader denounced from the pulpit. The color rose red in my cheeks.

"That Mirk dog I asked you about . . ." It seems Alasdair let Alan Gordon have him with the intention of buying him back but Alan Gordon sold Mirk to an American. "I would have bought Mirk back if Alan had told me." He talks about Mirk, what a wonderful dog he was. He wishes he had a Mirk pup today. All those grand bloodlines gone.

I am hiding in my bitter, but Alasdair, now he knows why I've come, has become cheerful and expansive. He tells me that his father is a well-respected fiddle player, that he plays as often as he wishes all the way to Fort William. "Everybody expected me to be as good a musician," he says. "If I had a son, I wouldn't expect him to be any good with the dogs."

Dinner came to just ten pounds. As we walked to the car in the gathering dusk, Alasdair says, softly, "I don't regret the things I did when I was drinking—though I did some silly things. I only regret selling Mirk to America. If I could walk onto the trial field with Mirk, oh, I'd be dangerous then."

Oddly, I was relieved I hadn't been able to buy Bute. I was honestly glad Alasdair wouldn't do the sensible thing with the unregistered black bitch and sell her. I didn't feel clever or competent, but I'm half used to that by now because I sleep like a baby.

In the morning Alasdair is quite helpful, suggests I visit Kenny Brehmer, gives me an address for John Angus MacLeod, asks me if I'll inquire about Mirk once I get home. I will. He says I can stop here again if I wish, that it wouldn't matter if he was here or no. "Just find yourself a bed."

Okay. I stand by my suitcases wishing I knew where to go. "Well . . ."

Alasdair cocks his head like a schoolmaster. He tells me about Davey McTeir. "You'll have heard of Davey," who'd been running J. M. Wilson's Bill dog until he and Wilson had a falling out and—just like that—Wilson reclaimed Bill. At the time Davey was strapped for cash. He had 150 pounds on the dresser, which he needed for something he'd promised—perhaps it was a car—for his family. But he heard of a young dog for sale: Ben. Davey spent the money for Ben. "A wise choice, eh Donald? A wise choice, eh?"

As it happened, that *was* a wise choice. McTeir's Ben was a wonderful dog. It wasn't a choice I would have made. I was middle-aged, and not at all dangerous.

I drove north on the west road, along Loch Ness, crawling behind the tourist coaches, edging past cars parked on the verge while tourists scanned Loch Ness with binoculars. While my clothes were being washed in Inverness, I drove out to Culloden Moor. There is not much to see. The battlefield where Charlie lost all is flat and not large. The spot where the clans charged, the English line held, the fatal English artillery thundered—a walker can tour the graveyard of the clans in an hour.

The Visitor's Centre displays an old-fashioned plaid with wrapping instructions in case anyone wants to try it on. They've relics of the battle: so and so's pistol, someone else's dirk. The original battle orders issued to Charlie's troops are there, as well as the forged version the English passed out to their own troops—the forgery with "No Quarter" added. Naturally, since the English were terrified of these barbarians, they fought hard and took revenge.

The highlanders were exhausted and hungry (they'd

had a biscuit, each, the day before), and Charlie ordered the Highland charge too late to be effective. They were outnumbered two to one: Charlie calculated every highlander was worth four English troops.

The duke of Cumberland, the English commander, was fat, ill natured, ugly, and victorious. He ordered no quarter, and most of the wounded highlanders were shot, a few were burned alive. Along Culloden footpaths are great upended boulders that mark where they buried the clans: Here the MacDonalds, here the Frasers. Here is the Well of the Dead where the English slew the wounded who dragged themselves to it for a last taste of cool water. A few tourists, dressed against the chill, stroll about taking pictures.

They fought in April, 240 years, twelve generations of men, ago, but the fighting seemed more recent than that. I wondered that the grass ripped by the rushing troops had time to heal. Today the Highland mists were very close to the earth, blanketing souls who might yearn to flee.

At Culloden, the Farquarson clan stood with Charlie. The MacCaigs stood with the Farquarsons.

With a 30,000-pound bounty on his head, Bonnie Prince Charlie wandered the western Highlands for half a year until a French ship took him off. Afterwards, he lived in Rome—a plump, unhappy man, cuckolded by his German wife, drinking too much, weeping openly when friends played Highland ballads in the long, long Italian evenings.

Cumberland's troops slaughtered the Jacobites. Those who escaped death on the battlefield were pursued to their own doorsteps and murdered there. Their homes were burned. New laws forbade the wearing of the tartan or playing the bagpipe. The highlanders were disarmed. Jacobite estates were confiscated by the Crown.

Although diehard Jacobites still hatched plots and Charlie never lost his place in the highlanders' hearts, the clans were done. After Culloden, many of the remaining chieftains began to discover London's charms and leased their lands to English sheep farmers, who signed their leases on condition that the land be untenanted. From 1746 until Victorian times, the small Highland farmers (crofters) were systematically driven off their holdings. Here and there in the Highlands, you'll find a mossy wall where a village used to be, a home's scorched lintel stone. Some crofters migrated to the shoreline, where they could make a scant livelihood gathering seaweed. Others moved south, crowding the warrens of Edinburgh and Glasgow. They arrived, already starving, distinguished by rural customs and dress, unskilled, speaking only Gaelic. They did not thrive. In 1835, life expectancy in Glasgow was about thirty years, fully half the children in some Highland parishes died by the age of eleven. Between 1780 and 1810, 42,000 highlanders left for Australia, the United States, and Canada. Four out of five survived the journey.

Although it wasn't that cold at Culloden, I was shivering when I got back to the car. I drove badly back through the tangled Inverness streets, and polite drivers blinked their warning lights at me. I was a sure thing for an accident and didn't dare the crowded Loch Ness road. I opted for the slower inland route south. The Bed and Breakfast in Fort Augustus was nicer than most. My room was smallish but Scandinavian modern, with a built-in writing desk. The owner was a fair-haired woman in her thirties. They'd run cattle previously, right on the shore of Loch Ness, but now they only kept tame Highland cattle for the tourists to photograph.

I said times were hard for American farmers, too. I said I'd just visited Culloden.

"Culloden was a sad day," she said.

I blustered, "But Charlie was such a twit!"

She was shocked, not by the sentiment, by the

word. "But it was *his,*" she said. "The throne was Charlie's by right."

"I'm from the wrong country to find arguments about thrones persuasive."

She looked at me. I coughed. I asked for a good place to eat. She directed me, adding, "will you be joining us for tea? Eight o'clock?"

"Sure," I mumbled, "Sure."

I was the only customer in the pub where I ate. The barmaid was friendly and had once read a book of mine. I scribbled an autograph on a bar napkin. The barmaid belonged to an environmental group fighting the introduction of salmon cages to Loch Ness. All that spilled fish feed and salmon manure would alter the lake's nutrient level and, besides, what about Nessie?

What if Nessie should find the tons of fresh salmon in their steel cage irresistible and damage herself in her attack? Or worse, what if she never attacked all? Think of all those lines of tourists waiting (but not forever) on the loch side.

Only a few B & Bs offered evening tea, and that was fine by me. Usually I gave it a miss. The Brits are more accustomed to group travel than Americans and seemingly have no problem meeting strangers in the evening after having met strangers all day. But I was feeling guilty about the "Charlie the twit" crack and put on my sport coat and tie to join the others.

The windows of the pine-paneled sitting room overlooked the loch. The blurry photograph on the grand piano beside the binoculars looked mighty like driftwood to me but, I suppose it *could* have been a slender neck. As we guests chatted softly, the light was falling on the loch. Our hostess was a teacher of the *ceidihl,* the Gaelic harp, and her young pupil was to travel to Edinburgh in the morning to audition for the Royal Academy of Music.

As Loch Ness turned black and gave itself over to its own deep creatures, a young girl, perhaps twelve, fingered the strings of a harp as tall as she was, creating a clattering gladsome greeting to the head of the Clan MacLeish and after, a plucked tune that hung in the air like smoke: a lament for Charlie.

There are Scots who'd feel foolish if they didn't take advantage of a fool. Late in life, when he certainly didn't need the money, J. M. Wilson sold his home, Whitehope, to a man who offered him far too much money. Even as he signed the papers, J. M. regretted the sale.

So there were dogs I could have bought for three thousand or so, dogs otherwise not for sale.

But if Scots are Calvinists, convinced that those predestined for heaven are prefigured by their earthly estates, they're Gaels, too, acquainted with brownies and ferlies, cantraips, spunkies, and fairies. In today's money, the reward for Prince Charlie was a half million dollars. Although Americans joke about Scots' tightfistedness, Charlie wandered the rough country for six months and no highlander claimed that reward.

I wasn't the only one seeking a good young bitch. Peter Hetherington was on the phone every week. Joe McRoberts was looking. Davey McTeir wanted a bitch to "put over the water."

I drove to Peebles, to Castle Douglas, to Kinross, to Dingwall, to Arcallader. I knew I should change the rental Ford's oil after three thousand miles, but. . . . On Saturdays and Sundays, I followed the sheepdog trials. At Gleniffer Braes, I watched from Peter Hetherington's car as the rain sluiced down and the windshield wipers cleared a triangle of faint vision and one at a time, hunched over, handlers got out of their cars to run their dogs. This trial was held beneath a convention of giant gray electrical transmission towers. Was this really my sport? What in God's name was I doing in this country? Half the time, I couldn't even understand the lingo. Would you spell that, please? Say again, please?

When I bought a collection of Bobbie Burns's poetry for the Lowland Scot's dictionary in the back, I made a good bargain. After a month among his countrymen, I could read a great poet I'd never kenned before. And Bobbie is a bonny companion, various enough for laughter, hard lust, drunkeness, and regret. Unlike most poets, Burns will accompany you everywhere.

Scotland was green, a dark, deep green like irrigated alfalfa fields at home. Mornings were usually misty or rainy, and all my photographs had a romantic flavor, wanted or not. I came to know and favor a few farmhouse B & Bs, and whenever I was near, that's where I headed in the late afternoons. I disliked the Scottish towns. The giants, Glasgow and Edinburgh, ate a week's supply of dwindling pound notes in a day. Midsize towns like Ayr and Kinross faced their high streets behind an unbroken wall of rectitude. The gardens behind the houses are lovely and quiet, but not for the traveler. Rooms on the High Streets echoed all night from lorry exhausts banging from one stone facade to the other.

I was confounded by Scottish distances. Villages, thirty miles apart on the map, I'd think: Okay, that's half an hour. But commuting ease wasn't a Scottish problem. Each village would be complete: its own post office and proper hotel, its grocer, newsagent, tearoom. And an hour on single track roads to get from one to the next.

Scotland is deeply invaded by the sea, and I was often ferried across sea lochs and firths, watching the countryside slide by, relaxed for a change as someone else took me to wherever it was I was going.

Young bitches?

"Aye, you should have seen it at the nursery finals.

The day after, fifteen dogs were put on the plane for America."

"I sell all my dogs to Scandinavia. All eye tested and x-rayed, oh they pay a frightful price."

Faithfully I read the dog ads in the *Scottish Farmer* and phoned up but each was sold, already gone. "Aye, the man came for her yesterday, sorry."

It was beginning to dawn on me there might not be a fine young bitch to win my heart, that I was hoping to luck into the same dog Scottish dog men spent a lifetime seeking. I wouldn't settle for a pup. There were plenty of promising pups in America. If I failed, I'd fail entirely.

Farmers were putting up their first growth alfalfa as silage and I hoped my own hay cutting, at home, was going well.

Dunoon is a short ferry ride from Port of Glasgow, and the town has been a working-class resort for years. There are plenty of confectioneries and gift shops, and the news agents sell tartan undershorts and postcards with jokes about Wee Willie and what is under a Scotsman's kilt. Scottish kitsch.

Down the peninsula, beyond the place where the road narrows, past the beautifully named hamlet, Toward, is the farm of Alasdair Mundell, a tall blackhaired man who's president of the Scottish Branch of the International Sheep Dog Society. In the sea loch below Alasdair's farm, two bulk liquefied gas freighters lie at anchor. They were built by the Dutch and are stored here unused. They are gray and big like naval vessels, and rust stains dribble below the anchor hawser.

"After they built them, the American cities wouldn't let them in," Alasdair explained.

The countryside is so fragile among hard international concerns.

Alasdair farms with his son Boyd, who tenants next door. The hills behind rise so abruptly, I had to crick my neck. I'd offered to help Alasdair with his work but wasn't unhappy he'd refused. Looking up that hill, I thought how my heart would pound, how I'd suck for air. Mundell's dogs' muscles are like stone. I asked about a young bitch in the byre, a young bitch named Liz. "Oh, she'll not be the one you're looking for," says Alasdair Mundell.

"Who's she from?"

"She'll be out of Templeton's Roy, but. . . ."

"Perhaps I could see her?"

The young, beautiful bitch was batty. When she was let off the lead, she thought she was free and ran about like a silly beast, only just controllable.

Boyd Mundell's Lynn bitch was scraggle tailed, boney, with half-flopped ears and no chest to speak of. "She's an old-fashioned collie," Boyd said with a grin. Lynn got beautiful when she worked; graceful, she gave the sheep the space to go where she wanted them. And Boyd was so fond of the homely wonderful bitch, I didn't have the heart to ask if he'd sell her.

Boyd's father had another new bitch, Meg, off the eminent Welsh sire, Bwlch (pronounced "Bulk") Taff. I liked Lynn much better than Alasdair's Meg, but in September, when I come back to Scotland for the International, Meg will have qualified for the great trial: Lynn won't have made the cut.

I had to trust my eyes, what else could I do? I had to believe that the right bitch would call out to me. But I felt a babe in the woods, depending on the Scot's restraint, their unflagging courtesy. That was what woke me in the middle of the night worrying. Where am I? Dunoon? I'd switch on the bedside lamp and read a couple of poems by Bobby Burns, who'd written *The Twa Dogs* after Luath, his Border Collie, was beaten to death, and who died himself before the age of forty.

In our culture, humans with a special knack for animals have always been thought queer, or worse. The witch's handiest allies were the beasts she summoned to do her bidding, and her familiar was always an unclean spirit in animal form. The idiot lad who alone can ride the killer stallion and gentles, with a touch, hurt mastiffs no one else dares approach—that lad is a staple of our fictions.

Since the Greeks, philosophers have answered our deep cultural need to separate ourselves from animals and famously have defined man as "just like other animals *but* rational, or tool making, or able to make promises or. . . ."

Western thought patterns have separated man from animals as surely as subject from verb and body from mind.

Learning a dog's worldview, altering it (within bounds), accepting a dog's understanding as sometimes more reliable than a man's—these commonplace tools of dog training are a mild cultural treason. The rare dog handlers who, by gift or necessity, become truly dangerous inhabit a reality most of us can scarcely imagine—every day they share the thoughts, habits, tics and aspirations of a genuinely alien mind. When I asked these men about their connection with their dogs, they were reticent. They were also, without exception, masterful and deeply obsessed.

Above Dunoon, along Holy Loch, where The United States provisions its nuclear submarines, Stuart Davidson has his modest, newish home. At the head of the loch rises the great hill farm Stuart manages and that's where Stuart showed me Craig and Moss, same way bred, both impeccable, powerful, bold.

Stuart has enough self-confidence. When he flew over to judge a big trial in the States, he disqualified his host's dog for gripping. "Oh, the man came up after to complain," Stuart says, bland as cream pie. He paused, letting me feel the weight of his competence. "Do you get to many trials then, Donald?"

"Aye."

One cocked eyebrow. "You're becoming a Scot yourself, eh?"

I blushed. Stuart's pretty young wife brought more tea. The trophy case in the neat sitting room was big around as a grown man, and it gleamed of silver and gold: bright plunder.

No, Stuart doesn't know of any good young bitches for sale. Bill Wyatt phones him from the States: "Get me the best," Bill says. "Money's no object."

Once more, Stuart raises an eyebrow.

Before I leave, I ask Stuart if it worries him, living so near ground zero—the first place the missiles would hit in the event of war. "You die if you worry, you die if you don't," he says.

I drive beside Holy Loch eyeing American nuclear subs. On the streets, U.S. Navy dependents shop for groceries. One angry looking young man is pushing a baby carriage. He wears a Texas hat, not unlike my own.

It has got to be a relief to sleep at the same B & B twice. Windy Hill Farm outside Strathaven is quiet, and I'm the only guest. When my hostess brings me tea and biscuits, she asks if I've found my bitch yet. "No ma'am, not yet."

I ring up the Templetons, and May Templeton says, yes, John'd love to see you, but he's going to the market and won't be back until afternoon.

"I've not seen a Scottish livestock market," I said. Perhaps I could tag along.

She was flustered. "John's planning to leave at eight."

"That'd be fine."

The Templetons's farm, Airtnock, was a brush heap in 1965 when they bought it. Although, early on, John had notable successes at the sheepdog trials, it was hard for him to leave May to manage everything on the farm. The minute John came off the course, he'd hop his dogs into the boot and go straight home.

Theses days, Airtnock boasts 100 milking Ayr-
shires, 250 sheep, and a herd of Limousin beef cattle.
John's able sons help out. Although John Templeton is
one of the most dangerous dog handlers to walk onto
the trial course, he makes his living as a dairyman.

This morning he's off to Lanark to sell a feeder
steer. "Oh," he says. "Don't bring your camera. It'll be
stolen."

Okay.

He also says, "Fasten your seat belt. It's our
law."

Okay.

He has the calm, pale face of a medieval saint,
someone whose concentration on salvation is absolute.
John is unfailingly polite. "Gilchrist Spot," he says,
"was too strong. Wiston Cap was mild and sulky, except when he was right and then nothing could touch
him."

"What about Jock Richardson?"

"He was a silly man."

I am accustomed to rough stateside livestock markets, where waiting stock trucks drool manure through
the racks and the farmers have come straight out of
the field—or at least their overalls have. American
farmers dress like men who are working themselves to
death, Scots like men who never lift a hand.

After we unload the steer, John hoses out the truck
box. "Oh yes," John says, "a wash is provided for the
transporters; it's our law."

The market is several barns and sale rings. Some,
like the octagonal sheep ring, are ancient. Farmers and
stock have stood under these skylights for a century. I
wished I had my camera. John Templeton shakes a few
hands and talks up his calf, "He's had a wee knock on
the ankle getting on the truck, but it'll soon be right."
After they're groomed, the calves are put in clean
straw-bedded pens.

Wearing a short white vet's coat, the auctioneer

stands above the sale ring, in a pulpit. "This is Mr. Jennings with his calf, a grand calf. One-fifty, do I have one-fifty? One-sixty, thank you sir; one-sixty, sixty; one-seventy, seventy; seventy-five; seventy-eight, seventy-eight (BANG); sold at one seventy-eight. Thank you, sir."

Each animal's farm is named. It is believed in Scotland that some farms always produce superior stock. In the States, animals come out by age or type or grade, pure hurly-burly. In the States buyers don't ask where a beast came from.

John Templeton's steer calf brings 226 pounds—not the top price, but not far below it.

The British are cutting back on milk production, and this day good Fresians come into the ring, their udders so full of milk some walk sideways. Many will go to Saudi Arabia. In the octagonal ring, lambs are being sold for slaughter, and butchers' boys stand right in the ring and feel the animals' backbones (chops) before they bid.

The Lanark Market restaurant has sturdy oak tables and waitresses dressed out of a 1940s movie, *The Harvey Girls*, perhaps. Middle-aged women in white aprons over black uniforms and lace caps bring respectable farmers their lasagna or steak and kidney pie.

John Templeton talks about other Americans who've come over. Arthur Allen at every International, taking notes on each dog that ran. "Oh he didn't like you talking to him." John pays.

Outside, farmers sell hay and eggs and live chickens and the only fresh produce I saw in Scotland.

John takes a different route home, past his uncle's farm near Sorn, where John got his start in sheepdogs. The ground is low, rolling hills, and though we passed through miners' villages, I saw no mines. This country provided the iron and coal that made Glasgow a great industrial center during the nineteenth century, but there's no evidence today it was ever anything but farmland.

John says good dogs are in great demand. Nearby, Hugh, a young dairy sheepman, has a Roy bitch that John fancies. John offered fifteen hundred pounds for her, but Hugh Ferguson wouldn't sell. John says Hugh has just bought himself a new estate wagon. Perhaps that fifteen hundred would come in handier now.

The farm above Templeton's was bought by the Forestry Commission which planted it in spruce. The spring which watered that farm and Airtnock waters others below, and when water is lacking, Airtnock, being highest, suffers first. Water is low now, but as we arrive, John, Junior, has just come out of the fields and is washing his tractor. Both the Templeton's tractors are newish, washed sparkling clean.

Like farms in northern New England, the outbuildings at Airtnock are contiguous, and the kitchen door opens on a low stone passageway into the old byre where they dogs are kept. I was glad to see that grand old dogs, now retired, are treated as well as the most promising young ones. John Junior's bitch, Di, is for sale. She's a pretty black and tan but will not meet my gaze.

The milking parlor is wet and steamy as a drive-through car wash, the cows on each side of a steel pit where John and John, Junior, connect and disconnect hoses for the milking machines. Raw milk pulses through clear plastic tubes to the bulk tanks.

After milking, John Templeton takes his Roy dog to the back pasture where he grazes his sheep. "There," John points to a sour tussocky field. "It was all like that when we first came here." He sends Roy for the sheep and as soon as the dog is well out, John commences a symphony of whistling.

This deluge of commands is John Templeton's controversial trademark. Many shepherds believe "the fewer commands the better" and, unless a dog has gone wrong, most issue no commands after they send a dog until the dog has brought the sheep to the man's feet. Fetching livestock (sheep or cows) is the Border Collie's simplest, most instinctive work and there are many routine American farm dogs that can't do anything else. They've never been taught to drive stock away from the man. The only part of a sheepdog trial where a man is penalized for commanding a dog is the outrun because it's thought the 'natural dog' will need no commands to gather his sheep. Probably this herding instinct was originally predatory. Perhaps the ancestral Border Collie was a small, clever beast, quick enough to outrun escaping prey and turn it back into the jaws of the pursuing pack.

In Australia, Border Collies are never taught to drive, and at their trials (which are quite different from the British-American variety), handlers are penalized any time the dog gets between the man and his sheep. The Australians fear that their bush-wild merino wethers can't be caught once the dog gets on the wrong side of them.

As Roy fetches his sheep at Airtnock, John Templeton never takes his eyes off him and whistles every step of the way. His whistles tumble over themselves like a bird song, quick, light, and happy. Roy is a sleek, black and tan, smooth-coated dog, at the top, or near the top of every Scottish National since he first started running, eight years ago. He and John are a famous combination.

John chirps as Roy makes split-second adjustments, perfectly balanced on his sheep, moving them with his eye.

(I fear this must seem easier and more comprehensible than it is. Go outside with one of your kids—your spouse won't stand for it—and try what John Templeton does with Roy: "Go right, go left, left, left, stop, walk up, lie down, right, go slow, left" *as* the child is concentrating on some delicate precise task, say, juggling three eggs in the air. Perhaps you thought what John and Roy did was pellucid: Man Commands, Dog Obeys. As you clean up broken eggs and dry your child's tears, you may recall that communion and communication intertwine at their roots.)

John Templeton is a master musician, creating a song that enthralls both John and Roy. The mind of man and dog is in that music.

It was another sort of music at the Chester International when Wiston Cap brought his sheep straight down the fetch line to Jock Richardson's feet, in uncanny silence, without command.

A bit later in the day, John, Junior, and I take Di out. Di won't be for sale long. Each time John Templeton Senior goes to America to judge a trial, he returns home with orders for well-bred dogs. And like Alasdair Mundell's new Meg bitch, Di is sired by Bwlch Taff. As we walk to a field with a few sheep, I am optimistic. Maybe Di'll meet my eyes when she knows me better.

Like his father, John, Junior, whistles constantly, commanding Di, commanding her. The outrun is a bit ragged, but acceptable, the fetch quite neat. She's a pretty thing too, and young.

"Would you please send her again without commands?"

"You'll nae be wanting to see her drive? She's got a good drive."

"Just the outrun and fetch please. No commands."

Without John, Junior's help, Di is a loose cannon. She races straight down the middle, panics her sheep into flight and scatters them. Her tail is flying like a foolish flag.

"She'll need settling," John, Junior, says.

"Aye. Just a little more training." That's me talking, noncommittal as any Scottish dog dealer. But it was antics you expected from a puppy, not a started dog, and her tail—oh dear.

As Jock Richardson says, "If the tail's no right, the dog's no right."

When a dog man comes to inspect the sheepdog you hope to sell, he likely won't care about coat length or color. Prick ears or flop ears? All the same. He will, invariably, stoop to look the dog in the eyes.

There are a good many theories about eye types: light versus dark brown; brown versus blue, but that's not what these men are looking for. They're looking into an honest dog's soul.

When the dog is tried on sheep, they'll want to see a wide, natural outrun and well-balanced fetch. They'll have the dog press tups into a corner until the tups turn and the dog must show courage. Just as the dog is concentrating hardest, they'll ask it to flank: to see if the dog is sticky.

A sticky dog can be loosened, a frightened dog given confidence, a tight-running dog can be widened out. But if the tail is set wrong, carried badly or afraid, it's No Sale.

The sheepdog's tail is his physical banner, emblem of his working habits and style. Foolish tail: foolish dog.

I do wish Di had been right. She was a pretty thing.

John Templeton has been on the Scottish Team at the International almost continuously since 1964. Team members' badges are modest gold rectangles, country and date: Scotland 1978, Scotland 1979. John Templeton's badges dangle in his trophy cabinet like battle honors on a general's chest.

May Templeton serves wine with supper, which is fine hospitality in a family that rarely drinks themselves. Later this year, she and John will fly to California to judge sheepdog trials. Who would have thought a small dog could put people across the Atlantic?

The Templetons' guest bedroom is spacious, old-fashioned, and comfortable. There's a guest book on the bedside table. There's a pen.

Downstairs the Templetons wait, nervously, for a call from their solicitor.

Last fall, they'd had a boundary fence built and, as is customary, they'd paid half the contractor's bill (May has the canceled check handy) and their fence-line neighbor was to pay the other half. The neighbor is flashy, drives flashy cars, won't return their phone calls, and has defaulted on his part of the bill. The angry fence contractor has said he's coming out tomorrow morning to pull the fence out.

In his comfortable slippers, in his own chair, before his home fire, John Templeton is desperately upset. May Templeton is confident, cheerful. In *The Symposium*, Plato created a beautiful metaphor of human love. He suggested that we humans once were unisex creatures, complete and happy, until we were ripped in two. Since that rough separation, men and women are condemned to wander the world looking for another being to make them whole. Some few pairs, like John and May Templeton, do make a whole, and it's impossible to imagine one without the other.

John's solicitor phoned the police to see if they'll intervene. May leans forward to explain, "John's a law-abiding man. He's not accustomed to this sort of thing."

In the morning, I leave before the fencing contractor makes his appearance. John and May scarcely notice me go.

At a smallholding near Sorn, I park beside Hugh Ferguson's new estate wagon.

The Fergusons are young, dressed in farm clothes that have seen plenty of hard work. John and May Templeton must have dressed like this when they first bought Airtnock. Their sheep dairy is (after the Templetons' automatic operation) primitive and slow. The ewes' teats are washed from a bucket of warm disinfecting water, and the pump is moved from ewe to ewe until each is done. The ewes, Hugh says, average 60 gallons per freshening, and he gets 42 pence a liter for the milk (which will be made into cheese). His greatest problem is transporting the milk to the cheese factory.

The best milk sheep are Frisians; the second best, Dorsets. Ferguson's ewes are handled daily and have no decent respect for a dog. Hugh's smooth-coated Maid bitch needs more work than the young man can give her—and wilder sheep, too. The pasture where Hugh works her is tussocky and rough.

I take Maid's picture. "I suppose she's not for sale."

There's the briefest, slightest hesitation before the young farmer says no.

I didn't press the matter, and later on, down the road, kicked myself. Tougher men than I might have persisted and got the bitch—and she was a topper. But I wasn't sure about offering sixteen hundred pounds, I didn't like the ethics of buying a dog away from John Templeton the day after enjoying his hospitality. Mostly, I thought that Maid was the only beautiful creature the Fergusons had.

At home, I am a creature of routine. Up at dawn, at chores by seven, back in the house for breakfast. Walk, train, feed the dogs. I hoped Pip was doing all right. He wouldn't give a damn if I came back from Scotland without a young bitch. I wasn't so sure I would give a damn myself.

I ran across Geoff and Viv Billingham, Saturday, at the Dalrymple trial. "Have you found her, Donald?"

"Nope. How are things at Tweedhope?"

"Oh smashing," Viv took my sleeve. "We've got the plumbing in and the Council's back at work on the layby."

Geoff asked if I'd been over to see the agricultural show, "They have some grand cattle, grand," but I was indifferent to the show, and the trial for that matter. I pulled my car to the far end of the parking lot and pulled my hat down over my eyes. Life had got to be too many for me.

When I came out of my fretful slumber, it was near noon and perhaps a third of the dogs had already run. I saw Holly run, but she was erratic. Not her day. I checked off the bitches listed in the program and when I looked up, the wee beast was on her fetch. I hadn't seen the outrun, but the fetch was quite nice; the young bitch kept well off her sheep and balanced them perfectly. *Gael—T. Reid*, the program read. The bitch brought the sheep around her handler's feet and started them to the drive gate. At the last moment, the sheep swerved and missed the gate, and the handler lifted his crook in the air: disqualified.

She was quite small, built sleek, smooth coated, black and tan. Powerful, like a .45 caliber pistol on a .38 frame. Gael lay at her handler's feet, cleaning her paws. Tom Reid, from Creetown. Near Newton Stewart, it is. "Aye," Tom Reid said, "Yin's a useful beast."

A man in his sixties, Reid wore a cap that matched his tweed jacket and the kind of tinted glasses Hollywood producers prefer. His lowlands accent was hard to understand. "She's two-and-a-half years. Aye, she ran at the nurseries, but I'm no a trial man, I'm a dog breaker [trainer]."

David McTeir made his appearance, and in the choreography of his arrival, I found myself shuffled to the rear, facing the backs of two men's tweed jackets. McTeir's face is a half size too big for his body, with the hard planes of an Easter Island carving. I'd met David before, but we didn't say hello today. Tom Reid and David McTeir spoke the lingo. It was their country. Their sport coats were more recently pressed than mine. "That's a bonny wee bitch." (David)

"Oh, aye. Aye." (Tom)

"And she'll keep off her sheep. I don't suppose she'd ever run too wide?" (David)

"Nae. She'd nae let a ewe get away from her." (Tom)

"And she'll kep [fetch] them right to you?" (David)

"Oh, aye." (Tom)

Pip.

Vic Billingham and Holly.

Whitehope.

The dogs of Tweedhope.

John Angus with Dougie.

The byre at Kiltyrie.

Mrs. David McTeir with tomorrow's champion.

John Templeton with Roy.

Jock Richardson at Neilston.

Alasdair MacRae with Bute.

Geoff Billingham with Cap.

Tom Reid with Gael.

Outside the beer tent.

John Templeton waiting his turn at the International.

Stuart Davidson at the International Brace Championship.

Just before the difficulties: John Angus with Taff.

Stuart Davidson and Moss at the pen.

The Duke of Atholl with the 1988 International Team.

John Angus McLeod.

Davie Sutherland with Bert and Bob.

"And with the tups, strong 'uns, she'd not be afeart of them?" (David)

"The wee bitch'll abide no nonsense. She'll nae grip. She's nae a grip in her. But she'll shift her sheep." (Tom)

As the two Scots traded these suppositions, they spoke softly, and if I hadn't been standing practically on their heels, I wouldn't have heard a word. Of course, it was rude to stay standing there. I stayed.

As David McTeir talked, he ran his crook gently down the wee bitch's back. She paid no mind but lay calmly watching the trial field.

"And how's she bred?"

"She's by MacKenzie's Don."

"Oh, aye. Grand hill dog, Don."

"She dinna just look her best today. She's just comin' off pups, ye ken."

She lay favoring her swollen teats. She was blowing her coat, and a wisp of hair rolled off her back in the faint breeze. Tom Reid coughed and held his handkerchief to his mouth. He said, "I only go to the local trials. Since I lost me leg [he patted his left leg] I dinna care to drive, so I must travel with others. They'll be anxious to be going."

McTeir persisted with his queries, "I suppose she'll go to either hand?"

"She didn't like her 'come bye' " (left flank). "She'd nae take it. So I said, I'll just breed her and see if that makes her go better, and now she'll go to either hand. And," he smiled, "I've four bonny pups in the bargain."

McTeir grew confidential, "I don't suppose you'd be selling her. Mind, I'm no a rich man."

"Oh, I have too many young dogs coming on. Perhaps."

"And what would you be asking?"

"Weel . . . after the nurseries, I turned down eight hundred pounds for her. Man wanted to take her to Ireland. But I have pups out of her now. . . ."

"Aye. Weel, I'm Davey McTeir. McTeir's Ben."

A smile of recognition. "Oh, aye. Aye."

". . . and Bill and Mirk."

"Oh aye. Famous dogs those."

"I'm looking for a bitch. Perhaps I'd come down and see how she goes at home."

As the two Scots exchanged phone numbers, I walked away. When I looked again, Davey McTeir was in conference with his friends, Tom Reid and the wee bitch were gone, and a long-haired dog was in difficulties on the trial course. Big dog. Looked like Pip, only bigger.

I felt the fool. The big white Texas hat I wore to the trials (just like I did in the States) was a fool's hat. I wished I spoke the language. In my mind's eye, I saw David McTeir run his stick down the wee bitch's back; gentle, idle, proprietary. In the car, I consulted my schedule. Trial tomorrow in Glenrothes. All the Highland handlers would be there. Maybe I could finally meet John Angus MacLeod. Glenrothes was a long haul, across the Firth of Forth from Edinburgh. If I was to find a B & B at Glenrothes, I should phone ahead for a reservation. On the Dalrymple course, a Scot was running a dog better than I owned, better than I would have run him. The Billinghams had gone home. The sun shined down. Oh, it was a bonny day for an agricultural fair.

In the beer tent I asked for a whisky. I poured water from the cool pitcher. The barman returned 20 pence from my pound note. "How far to Creetown?"

The barman shook his head, "I'm afraid I dinna ken it." He turned to his assistant, "Mary, have ye ever hear't of a place, 'Creetown'?"

She shook her head. "It'll no be near here."

"Newton Stewart?"

"Oh aye. That'd be well south. Ayint Stranraer."

I took out my notebook. "Would you spell that, please?"

On my map, Newton Stewart looked like fifty miles. The dash clock said 4 P.M. I hoped Creetown was small enough so I could find Tom Reid. I drove dangerously, like a bat out of hell.

At 6 P.M., I stopped in Newton Stewart and I popped coins into a phone box. I got Reid's number, but it buzzed and buzzed.

The parking lot behind the Creetown Arms was such a tight turn that I had to take two shots at it. The dusk had turned odd, cold, and there was no greenery in this place and never had been. So near the coast, I could smell the sea iodine in the air.

Robert, my host, was a middle-aged Englishman who'd sold the hotel but was managing it until the new owners came in. Robert dreamed of owning a regular pub somewhere in the south. "At closing time you are finished," he said. "No more bother. Close the door, sweep up, go to bed."

Creetown, he said, was not lively. The young man sitting at the bar nodded agreement: Though he was born here, he and his wife lived in London now. No, he didn't know any Tom Reid. "A sheepdog man, you say? George, have you heard of Tom Reid?"

George, a dour old herd, shook his head.

"George herded here since before I was born," the young man confided. "He knows everybody."

Gloomily, George consulted his pint. I had another myself. The young man, it turned out, was a prison warder. "Oh, the work's not too bad. The pay's all right." That's right, he was home for a visit. His uncle had sheepdogs, perhaps the American had heard of him?

"No, I'm afraid not."

"Oh, he sells his pups as far as Castle Douglas. Gets fifty pounds for them." Uncle raised purebred tups, perhaps the American had heard of them? His tups brought fabulous money, last year one fetched twenty-seven thousand pounds. "Do you know how you can tell a good sheepdog?" he asked.

No, I didn't.

The prison warder opened his mouth and pointed his finger in there. "Black mouth," he advised. "The roof of its mouth'll be black. That's what Uncle told me. If you want a gude sheepdog, you must open its mouth."

I tried to phone Tom Reid but still no answer.

Robert said, "That's a Newtown Stewart exchange."

"That's why we dinna know him," the young warder said. "He's no in Creetown."

"Uh-huh." I had a pint. The clock made its rounds. I ate lasagna. Some of Creetown's unmarried young came in for a drink before they went dancing. Like country young everywhere, they were dressed in a pastiche of recent urban fashions. The boys' pants were too tight, and I wouldn't have wanted to walk far in their sharp flimsy shoes. The girls wore bright blouses that had been ironed fresh that afternoon.

When Reid answered the phone, I was suddenly at a loss. I'd almost given him up for an evening in the pub. "Mr. Reid?"

"Aye."

"I'm the American you talked to at Dalrymple today. I was wondering if I could come by and look at your wee bitch?"

Long pause. "We'el, you know there's a man interested in her. Mister McTeir. Famous for the dogs."

"I'm in Creetown. I drove all the way down here just to see her."

"Oh aye . . . Well, she's not my only bitch, you know. I've a three year old ready to trial."

"So you wouldn't mind if I came over?"

"Oh, I suppose not." Tom Reid gave directions.

As I came down Carswilloch Farm lane, it was nine

o'clock, the light plummeting into dark. The farm was flat. The land behind it was flat, too, until it ran up against the blunt black horizon. Tom Reid stood outside his modest cottage, beyond the darkened main house, beyond the equipment shed. I shook his reluctant hand briskly.

"Aye. Now, like I told you when you rang, Mr. McTeir has expressed an interest. He'll be coming by to see her."

"Uh-huh. But I'm here now. You haven't sold her, have you?"

"Nae." A pause. "Where are you from in the States?"

"Virginia. It's the state right behind Washington, D.C., on the television news."

"Oh aye. We'el she's fed her pups and her belly's full of meat. . . ."

"I'm sure she'll be fine."

"I've another bitch, that's ready to trial. . . ."

"Oh, that wee bitch, she's a . . . bonny beast."

Sighs. "Aye. We'el, there's tups down the road I have the use of. . . ."

"We can take my car."

The wee bitch wasn't at all keen to come out of her doghouse. "Come along, lassie. Come along now." Tom Reid unclipped the chain from the doghouse and used it as a lead. "She doesn't care for the car. When she was eighteen month she was in a smashup. She always rode between my wife's feet. My wife's deid."

When we got to the training field, the only light was a thin band on the horizon. The field was ten acres, kidney shaped, bordered by trees. At the far end were gray shapes—a half dozen of them. "Could you have her fetch them without commands?"

A look. "Aye."

She sailed out, came to the treeline, raced along it, stopped. Tom Reid whistled two sharp whistles, and the wee bitch disappeared into the dark. I couldn't see her now, but the gray shapes began to flock together. The bitch was a presence, like a negative magnet behind them. They came: big beasts, unshorn Cheviots, swathed in thick battings of wool.

"Gael! Take time, Gael!"

And the Cheviots slowed. The wee bitch was flanking from one side to the other, keeping just far enough off the sheep so she wouldn't panic them. "Could you ask her to circle around them to the left?" I asked.

"Come bye, Gael."

The wee bitch came to their faces and they jolted to a stop like rail cars run into a yard bumper.

"Bring her around to the right."

She did that, too. "It's getting hard to see. . . . Would you have her press them against the fence?"

"Aye." The older man had got into the spirit of demonstrating his dog. When he asked the wee bitch to press the tups against the fence, they'd have no escape, they'd turn on her, drop their heads, stamp. "Get up, lassie. That's a girl. Get up, lassie!"

She hesitated but came on to those snorting pawing 250-pound tups, lifting her forepaw, setting it down, leaning forward onto it, sliding, like a drawer on a glide.

"Flank her, please."

In the dark, she flashed back and forth under the tups' noses, left, then right, then left again, and you could tell where she was because all the tups aimed at her.

"That's all I needed to see," I said.

Tom Reid called Gael to his side. He said, "Her outrun was no right just then. But she was asleep when we fetched her and her belly is full of meat. . . ."

"I'll give you eleven hundred pounds for her."

Though the field at our feet was perfectly dark, there was enough light higher, for Reid and me to see each others' faces. "Ach, weel. Mister McTeir, he'll be coming to look at her. We'd exchanged phone numbers." Tom Reid stooped to reattach the clumsy kennel chain.

"You know and I know David McTeir isn't going to keep her. He'll sell her to somebody else for more than he pays you. I'll take her home with me. There's no difference between me and David McTeir except you'll know who's got her, where her home is."

Reid inspected me for about thirty seconds. He said, "Let's go back to the cottage. Do ye have much dog trialing in the States?"

On our drive, I made conversation, "You're a hard man to get ahold of," I said. "Nobody in Creetown seemed to know you."

"My wife and I moved here in the summer. She was already sick with the cancer." In the glare of my headlights, Tom Reid led the wee bitch into her doghouse. Gratefully, she scooted inside and lay down, facing away. Tom Reid sighed. "She's had a hard day, poor best. The pups take it out of them. Come inside, man. What would you be saying to a wee dram?"

We sat in overstuffed armchairs on either side of an electric fire. Family snapshots reposed on the sideboard. Tom Reid found his whisky and hobbled into the kitchen for water. The framed photograph on the wall must have been three feet long: sheepdog in working stance. The photo bore the legend: "Don—Breeder: J. Herries, Trainer: T. Reid, Owner: J. Varnon."

"Mister Varnon sent me that picture from Texas. He was that pleased with Don. Have ye seen Don?" Tom Reid asked.

"No, he's in Texas. I don't get that far south."

"Don was a topper. I sold him to Peter Hetherington. Do ye ken Peter?"

"Uh-huh."

"I don't doubt Peter made a few quid when he put Don to America." He rubbed his knee. "Ach, it aches when I'm in a car so long. After Dalrymple, we stopped for a blether on the way." He poured another half tumbler of whisky. "Ye'll have dogs at home, then?"

I said I couldn't farm without Pip, but when I ran

in the sheepdog trials, nobody worried when I walked to the post.

"I've been a herd all me life, but I'm no hand at the trials me sel."

I eased up. Pleasant fire. Good whiskey. How had I thought Scots were hard to understand? I said, "When I think of the dogs, it isn't the trials. I value them for what they do at home."

It happened last spring. Full-moon night. I was undressing for bed when a car started honking up on the road. My wife said, "The lambs are out."

So long as nobody brought up that subject, bed was still a possibility. "Pip," I called.

The Virginia State Road was the upper border of our farm. Above the road were eighteen thousand acres of unfenced, roadless, wooded Bullpasture Mountain: State Game Commission land. Sheep climb when they're confused or afraid, and last fall my wife and I spent days up there scouring the rough ground for missing sheep.

I drove down the road with my lights off, looking for the lambs in the road, hoping to intercept them before they started up the mountain. Pip sat in the passenger's seat, peering out the window. When I stopped the car, twenty lambs clambered through the fence back down into the field, but when Pip and I got out, there was no way of knowing whether all the lambs had gone back in or if others were farther down the road or up the mountain. There was a muddle of hoofprints and droppings on the hard dirt road. I drove along slowly until I reached the steel bridge, the farthest the lambs would have gone, parked, and Pip and I walked back below the great looming mountain. Nobody else lives in that valley, and there were no lights and no cars. The glaucous moon shone on the low fog below. I kept my flashlight in my pocket.

Whenever I came to a hollow that'd take lambs up the mountain, I asked Pip to inspect it. "No, Boss. The sheep haven't gone up here."

The moon was very beautiful, the fog swirled. When I paused again, Pip assured me the sheep hadn't gone up here either.

Beyond the farm's east boundary is a decaying log house and a handful of ruined piebald apple trees. Tufts of wool clung to the torn fence. Below lay three hundred acres of ill-kempt ground between the road and the river.

I told Pip, "Go down there on the right hand and see if you find anything."

Hunkered on that moonswept road above the ocean of fog, I waited ten minutes before Pip came back to report: no sheep. Pip's tongue was hanging out. He was a very happy dog.

I asked my dog to go out to the left, around the old log house, and look for sheep there.

After a quarter hour, Pip emerged from the fog and told me there weren't any lambs down there anywhere. Satisfied, man and dog went home. I'd fix the fence in the morning.

Tom Reid filled my glass. He said, "You don't want to get caught by our police, drinking and driving. They'll have your license for it."

I said it wasn't too far to my hotel.

"Will ye pay cash?" Tom Reid asked.

"Sure."

"I know that McTeir. He'll come over to the house and say, 'Oh, I don't know.' Just working at the price you see." Tom Reid leaned forward, past the fire. "I'm thinking I'll let ye have the bonnie wee bitch," he said.

I thought I already had her. It took me aback that the other man had been making up his mind as I talked about Pip.

"Ye'll write? I'll want to hear about her."

"Yes. I'm sure she'll do well."

"We'll hope she will. But I'll want to hear whether she does well or ill."

I said I'd send photographs. "It's pretty where we live. All the hills are timbered." I'd find out where to get Gael's eyes tested. PRA (progressive retinal atrophy) and CEA (collie eye anomaly) occur often enough to be wary of them.

Tom Reid said, "Our bargain depends on the eye test?"

"Aye," I said.

"Ach weel," he eased his wooden leg.

When I took Tom's hand this time, it was firm. Handshakes in Scotland are for sealing bargains, not for howdy-dos.

On the way back to the hotel, I kept an eye out for police cars but didn't see any. I had a hard time squeezing into the hotel car park.

"Did you find your man then?" Robert, the hotel keeper asked.

"And the bitch. Drinks on me."

In Montana, drinks for the house are a celebratory custom. This custom, though unknown in Scotland, was not unwelcome and served the same purpose: I met everybody. "So you like her?"

"Oh, she's bonnie. Very wee. She won't weigh thirty-five pounds."

"Did ye get a look at her mouth?" the prison warder pointed into his open mouth, which was pink. "A gude sheepdog'll have a black mouth."

"Sure."

It turned out everybody knew Carswilloch Farm where Tom Reid was living. Carswilloch Farm was the famous tup farm they'd talked about earlier.

"He canna have been there long," the warder said, shaking his head. "I'll ask me uncle about him."

The young people who'd been in earlier returned for a nightcap. Robert, the hotel keeper, bought a pint and I returned the favor. Back and forth it went.

The next morning, over breakfast in the Creetown Arms, I realized I'd spent eleven hundred pounds (nineteen hundred dollars) for a dog I'd seen for five minutes at a trial and subsequently in the dark.

Hung over, I pottered back up the coast to Ayr. There were public phones in Ayr where I could call my wife and let her know about the bitch.

I'd spent less than nineteen hundred dollars on my farm truck.

I crossed into Ayr on an ancient stone footbridge and wondered they hadn't torn it down. Like all Scottish towns, there was a decently clean public loo in the middle of town and signs pointing to it. (What few public toilets American cities have are well hidden for fear the wrong sort will gather there. Americans would not be thought sexual fools.)

I didn't phone my wife after all. She'd be sure to ask questions about the bitch. The Glasgow Veterinary School said yes, indeed, there's an eye specialist coming in: Tuesday, a week. I asked where I could catch the specialist sooner, and the vet school said he'd be in England. England seemed very far. It is not Scotland. It is a foreign land.

There're more handlers at Dalrymple the second day of the trial. I ask John Templeton how it turned out with the fence contractor, and he says it was all right, the neighbor coughed up his share. I say I've found my bitch.

"Who had her?"

"Tom Reid. Reid. He's no trials man. A dog breaker, that's what he is."

John Templeton's face was blank.

"That's him over there. With those three others. He's the man with the tinted glasses. He's got a bad leg."

"Oh him." Templeton made a face. "That man'd sell anything. He'd sell his shoes."

I said something about how well she'd gone last night, how she was a "bonny wee bitch," but the words sounded stagey in my mouth.

John Templeton said, "Excuse me. I'll be running next."

"Oh, sure. Sure." When John Templeton jumped his dog out of the car, I asked, "Now, which dog is that?"

The dog was Roy, the distinctively marked dog I'd watched at Neilston ... and Kinross ... and Airtnock. . . .

"Roy," John said, and turned away.

Tom Reid stayed deep among his friends. Their uniforms were wellies, waterproofs, weary sports jackets. Reid was, by far, the sharpest dressed and didn't introduce me to anyone. I explained about Glasgow and eye testing, and it all seemed a complex, difficult notion. Reid's dialect had thickened overnight, and I said, "Sorry?" and "Say again?"

Reid said he got *his* dogs tested when the vets came to the trials during the regular season. I said a week from Tuesday was long enough to wait. "I'll drive you," I said.

"Ach weel." Reid said he'd like to get his other bitch, his trial bitch, tested, too.

I said sure, I'd make that appointment as well. I wished Reid had brought the bonny wee bitch today. I was dying for another look at her. I really wanted to ask Reid if he sold a great many dogs but feared his answer. "Tuesday morning," I said. "I'll pick you up. Not this week, next week."

I drove deeper into the countryside, no place in mind, taking the smaller road at every junction.

The Black Bull Hotel in Straiton was booked up, sorry. Wedding party. I hoped that was true. I was sick: white faced and sweat greasy and substandard. Outside town I found a horse farm that took guests, and upstairs, in my small clean room, at two o'clock I climbed into bed and didn't get up until seven the next morning.

5

Sirrah

For a week I played tourist. Wednesday daybreak, no other soul in sight, I waded a tidal flat to the hulk of Castle Tioram. Gray-black stones clung to the sharp outcrop like a smashed barnacle. Outside, the redoubt was big and strong and I would have been afraid to attack it. Inside, it was cramped, scarce room for the fear and sweat and woodsmoke of those huddled here for protection while, across the sea loch, oily plumes told which hovels had been fired.

All over Scotland are sites where men tossed their lives away, gaily, for passions that are, today, incomprehensible. Usually men think their rulers know more than they do. Sometimes sheepdogs think so. Invariably, sheep do.

I drove to Killin in the Central Highlands and finally met the man other Scots had been pointing me towards: John Angus MacLeod. I spent a strange and unsettling weekend following John to the trials.

Next Tuesday, if Gael failed her eye exam, I'd be off the hook: "Terribly sorry, Mr. Reid. Glad to have met you. Too bad we couldn't strike a bargain."

Why hadn't I taken time to inspect her, deliberately, in the daylight? Had I been so very desperate? Why hadn't I seen the signs? Reid's too sharp clothes, his tinted glasses, his polished dealer's shoes?

I'd been blinded by the dream of a great dog.

Maybe that's why I stopped in Hamilton to see Jock Richardson again. Although the local pub was the roughest I'd seen in Scotland, furniture that had been used as weapons in bar brawls, a sign that said, simply NO FOOTBALL COLOURS PERMITTED; council housing across the road was neat enough and the Richardsons' duplex had flowers bordering its postage stamp front yard. Jock was in shirtsleeves—a vaguely smiling big man with no belt and his waistband turned inside out. "I do the vegetables," he confessed. "It's Mary does the flowers."

He didn't know why I'd come, he was no longer on the Hill, his great dogs were all dead, but Jock's courtesy ran deep and he showed me into the parlor and Mary brought tea while he ruffled through the boxes that held his clippings and awards. "Mary, where's Cap's papers?"

He spoke about Sweep, a big black dog, very powerful with sheep: "If he couldn't wear [bring] them to you, Sweep could practically carry them." Wiston Cap? Cap made Jock confident when he went to the post.

Atop the trophy case, above the neglected, unpolished trophies, a photo showed Jock and Cap in their prime. Jock wears the bemused smile of a man who finds himself, briefly, immortal. Cap is smiling too.

Tied in the shed out back, Jock's got a young dog. Yes, yes, he's Cap breeding, two years old. No, Jock hasn't trained him, he has no sheep.

The dog is strong chested and is desperately keen and Jock makes a slight motion of his hand and the young dog is glad to drop like a stone.

"A pity," Jock says.

I think of the lovely, intricate conversations they will never have. I agree that yes, yes, it is a pity.

Later that afternoon, I went into a library to read James Hogg's account of his grand dog, Sirrah.

It is all regrets.

I

SCOTLAND, 1803

My dog was always my companion. I conversed with him the whole day—I shared every meal with him, and my plaid cloak in the time of a shower; the consequence was, that I generally had the best dogs in all the country. The first remarkable one that I had was named Sirrah. He was beyond all comparison the best dog I ever saw. He was of a surly unsocial temper—disdained all flattery and refused to be caressed; but his attention to his master's commands and interests never will again be equalled by any of the canine race. The first time that I saw him, a drover was leading him in a rope; he was hungry, and lean, and far from being a beautiful cur, for he was all over black, and had a grim face striped with dark brown. The man had bought him of a boy for three shillings, somewhere on the Border, and doubtless had used him very ill on his journey. I thought I discovered a sort of sullen intelligence in his face, notwithstanding his dejected and forlorn situation, so I gave the drover a guinea for him, and appropriated the captive to myself. I believe there never was a guinea so well laid out; at least, I am satisfied that I never laid out one to so good purpose. He was scarcely then a year old, and knew so little of herding that he had never turned sheep in his life, but as soon as he discovered that it was his duty to do so, and that it obliged me, I can never forget with what anxiety and eagerness he learned his different evolutions. He would try every way deliberately, till he found out what I wanted him to do, and when once I made him to understand a direction, he never forgot or mistook it again. Well as I knew him, he often astonished me, for when hard pressed in accomplishing his task, he had expedients of the moment that bespoke a great share of the reasoning faculty. Were I to relate all his exploits, it would require a volume; I shall only mention one or two, to prove what kind of an animal he was.

I was a shepherd for ten years on the same farm, where I had always about 700 lambs put under my charge every year at weaning time. As they were of the short, or black-faced breed, the breaking of them was very ticklish and difficult task. I was obliged to watch them night and day for the first four days to prevent them from rejoining their mothers. During this time, I always had a lad to assist me. It happened one year, that just about midnight the lambs broke loose, and came up the moor upon us, making a noise with their running louder than thunder. We got up and waved our cloaks and shouted, in hopes to turn them, but we only made matters worse, for in a moment they were all round us, and by our exertions we cut them into three divisions; one of these ran north, another south, and those that came up between us, straight up the moor to the westward. I called out, "Sirrah, my man, they're a' [all] away;" the word, of all others, that set him most upon the alert, but owing to the darkness of the night, and blackness of the moor, I never saw him at all. As the division of the lambs that ran southward were going straight towards the fold, where they had been that day taken from their dams, I was afraid they would go there and again mix with them, so I threw off part of my clothes, and pursued them, and by great personal exertion, and the help of another old dog that I had besides Sirrah, I turned them, but in a few minutes afterwards lost them altogether. I ran here and there, not knowing what to do, but always, at intervals, gave a loud whistle to Sirrah, to let him know that I was depending on him. By that whistling, the lad who was assisting me found me out, but he likewise had lost all trace whatsoever of the lambs. I asked if he had never seen Sirrah? He said he had not, but that after I left him, a wing of the lambs had come round him with a swirl, and that he supposed Sirrah had given them a turn, though he could not see him for the darkness. We both concluded, that whatever way the lambs ran at first, they would finally land at the fold where they left their mothers, and without delay, we bent our course towards that; but when we came there there was nothing of them nor any kind of bleating to be heard, and we discovered with vexation that we had come on a wrong track.

My companion then bent his course towards the farm of Glen on the north, and I ran away westward for several miles, along the wild tract where the lambs had grazed while following their dams. We met after it was day, far up in a place called the Black Cleuch, but neither of us had been able to discover our lambs, nor any traces of them. It was the most extraordinary circumstance that had ever occurred in the annals of the pastoral life! We had nothing for it but to return to our master and inform him that we had lost his whole flock of lambs and knew not what was become of one of them.

On our way home, however, we discovered a body of lambs at the bottom of a deep ravine, called the Flesh Cleuch, and the indefatigable Sirrah standing in front of them, looking all around for some relief, but still standing true to his charge. The sun was then up; and when we first came in view of them, we concluded that it was one of the divisions of the lambs, which

Sirrah had been unable to manage until he came to that commanding situation, for it was about a mile and a half distant from the place where they first broke and scattered. But what was our astonishment when we discovered by degrees that not one lamb of the whole flock was wanting! How he had got all the divisions collected in the dark is beyond my comprehension. The charge was left entirely to himself from midnight until the rising of the sun, and if all the shepherds in the Forest had been there to assist him, they could not have effected it with greater propriety. All that I can say further is, that I never felt so grateful to any creature below the sun as I did to Sirrah that morning.

I remember another achievement of his which I admired still more. I was sent to a place in Tweeddale, called Stanhope, to bring home a wild ewe that had strayed from home. The place lay at the distance of about fifteen miles, and my way to it was over steep hills, and athwart deep glens; there was no path, and neither Sirrah nor I had ever travelled the road before. The ewe had been caught and put into a barn over night; and, after being frightened in this way, was set out to me in the morning to be driven home by herself. She was as wild as a roe, and bounded away to the side of the mountain like one. I sent Sirrah on a circular route wide before her, and let him know that he had the charge of her. When I left the people at the house, Mr. Tweedie, the farmer, said to me, "Do you really suppose that you will drive that sheep over these hills, and out through the midst of all the sheep in the country?" I said I would try to do it. "Then, let me tell you," said he, "that you may as well try to travel to yon sun." The man did not know that I was destined to do both the one and the other! Our way, as I said, lay all over wild hills and through the middle of flocks of sheep. I seldom got a sight of the ewe, for she was sometimes a mile before me, sometimes two; but Sirrah kept her in command the whole way—never suffered her to mix with other sheep—nor, as far as I could judge, ever to deviate twenty yards from the track by which he and I went the day before. When we came over the great height towards Manor Water, Sirrah and his charge happened to cross it a little before me, and our way lying down hill for several miles, I lost all traces of them, but still held on my track. I came to two shepherd's houses, and asked if they had seen anything of a black dog, with a branded face and a long tail, driving a sheep? No, they had seen no such thing, and, besides, all their sheep, both above and below the houses, seemed to be unmoved. I had nothing for it but to hold to my way homeward; and at length, on the corner of a hill at the side of the water, I discovered my trusty coal-black friend sitting with his eye fixed intently on the burn below him, and sometimes giving a casual glance behind to see if I was coming; he had the ewe standing there, safe and unhurt.

When I got her home, and set her at liberty among our own sheep, he took it highly amiss. I could scarcely prevail with him to let her go; and so dreadfully was he affronted that she should have been let go free after all his toil and trouble that he would not come near me all the way to the house, nor yet taste any supper when we got there. I believe he wanted me to take her home and kill her.

He had one very laughable peculiarity, which often created no little disturbance about the house—it was an outrageous ear for music. He never heard music but he drew towards it; and he never drew towards it but he joined in it with all his vigour. Many a good psalm, song, and tune he spoiled; for when he set fairly to, at which he was not slack, the voices of others had no chance with his. It was customary with the worthy old farmer with whom I resided to perform family worship evening and morning; and before he began, it was always necessary to drive Sirrah to the fields and close the door. If this was at any time forgot or neglected, the moment that the psalm was raised he joined with all his zeal, and at such a rate, that he drowned the voices of the family before three lines could be sung. Nothing further could be done till Sirrah was expelled. But then! when he got to the peat-stack knoll outside the door, especially if he got a blow in going out, he did give his powers of voice full scope, without mitigation, and even at that distance he was often a hard match for us all.

Some imagined that it was from a painful sensation that he did this. No such thing. Music was his delight; it always drew him towards it like a charm. I slept in the byre-loft—Sirrah in the hay nook in a corner below. When sore fatigued, I sometimes retired to my bed before the hour of family worship. In such cases, whenever the psalm was raised in the kitchen, which was but a short distance, Sirrah left his lair; and laying his ear close to the bottom of the door to hear more distinctly, he growled a low note in accompaniment, till the sound expired: and then rose, shook his ears, and returned to his hay-nook. Sacred music affected him most; but in either that or any slow tune, when the tones dwelt upon the key-note, they put him quite beside himself; his eyes had the gleam of madness in them; and he sometimes quitted singing, and literally fell to barking.

The most painful part of Sirrah's history yet remains; but in memory of himself, it must be set down. He grew old, and unable to do my work by himself. I had a son of his coming up that promised well, and was a greater favourite with me than ever the other was. The times were hard, and the keeping of them both was a tax upon my master which I did not like to impose, although he made no remonstrances. I was obliged to part with one of them; so I sold old Sirrah to a neighbouring shepherd for three guineas. Sirrah was accustomed to go with any of the family when I ordered him and run at their bidding the same as at my own; but then, when he came home at night, a word of approbation from me was recompense sufficient, and he was ready next day to go with whomsoever I commanded him. Of course, when I sold him to this lad, he went away when I ordered him, without any reluctance, and wrought for him all that day and the next as well as ever he did in his life. But when he found that he was abandoned by me, and doomed to be the slave of a stranger for whom he did not care, he would never again do another feasible turn. The lad said that he ran in among the sheep like a pup, and seemed intent on doing him all the mischief he could. The consequence was, the lad was obliged to part with him in a short time; but he had more honour than I had, for he took him to his father, and desired him to foster Sirrah, and be kind to him as long as he lived, for the sake of what he had been; and this injunction the old man faithfully performed.

Sirrah came back to see me now and then for months after he went away, but afraid of the mortification of being driven from the farmhouse, he never came there; but knowing well the road that I took to the hill in the morning, he lay down near to that. When he saw me coming he did not venture near me, but walked round the hill keeping always about 200 yards off, and then returned to his new master again, satisfied for the time that there was no more shelter with his beloved old one for him. When I thought how easily one kind word would have attached him to me for life, and how grateful it would have been to my faithful old servant and friend, I could not help regretting my hard fortune that obliged us to separate. That unfeeling tax on the shepherd's dog, his only bread-winner, has been the cause of much pain in this respect. The parting with old Sirrah, after all that he had done for me, had such an effect on my heart, that I have never been able to forget it to this day.

II

SIRRAH IN HEAVEN

I interviewed the handsome, black, rough coated beast on the heights of Broad Law, above Meggat Water, in early September. Although I'd arranged with Sirrah to meet at daybreak, I had some slight difficulty finding heaven and by my arrival at the foot of Broad Law, the sun was well up and Sirrah away on his morning gather. Though I am accustomed to hard walking, Broad Law is a painfully steep slope; my jersey was tied at my waist and perspiration had created a collar round my neck long before I attained the old bucht (sheepfold) Sirrah had approved for our meeting. Despite the cruel grade, the slope was often interrupted by freshets, and when I took breath on the infrequent narrow terraces, my feet sank into peat moss and water bubbled over my shoes. The weather was uncertain, and bold clouds skated across the autumnal sky. My bulky tape recorder clapped against my hip and snagged in the thickets of bracken. Away to the east, Dollar Law was streaked with purple heather. A duet of oyster catchers swooped around me, curious at my presence on this vertical moor where only collie dogs and shepherds commonly ventured.

The bucht was a rude enclosure of mortared stone with a chest-high gate on wooden hinges, these weathered gray as the stone itself. A bar of darker wood slid through the gate into a recess in the stone and thus secured the passageway.

The bones at the forefront of my cranium strained and thumped from my vertical exertions, and my nose ran copiously. Gratefully, I sprawled on a great stone slab the bucht's builders had found too unmanageable to incorporate into their structure. Very far below, mists attended the head of Meggat Water, and as they swirled this way and that, the sun glanced against them and brushed them spun gold. That dot in the sky, a hand's span from the sun, might have been a harrier hawk, searching the bleak landscape for a vole or small hare. Nits on nearby Black Law I thought to be roe deer, though they might as easily have been sheep. The sun had graciously warmed the stone wall at my back.

It became apparent that I had damaged my recorder during my climb, for when I executed a routine test, the machine and its instruments lay mute and motionless in my lap. I'd thought the batteries were fresh, but evidently had been mistaken. Thus, the reader interested in the details Sirrah related must rely on notes I made at the time and my recollections, transcribed subsequently.

When Sirrah first swung into sight, he followed a narrow footpath that coursed the hill below the old bucht. This footpath would have been indistinguishable from just yards away, but Sirrah had traveled it so habitually that he spared it not a glance. Instead, his attention was riveted down the slope, where, shortly, a group of some three-score ewes came into sight, attended by another, younger dog who bore a strong resemblance, I fancied, to Sirrah himself.

Although the younger dog had his sheep well in hand, marching them along in a fluid, steady manner, the elder dog's countenance bore a critical cast, like a master unsatisfied with an apprentice's work that is not quite up to the mark. The sheep were blackface yearlings in moderate fleece.

Although Sirrah spied me the moment he hove into sight, except for that single glance, he reserved his gaze for the sheep until they were well away and around the next shoulder of the hill. He then alloted me a second, scarcely lengthier inspection and a grimace, insufficiently concealed, before he bent to a pool of spring water and lapped his fill.

Sirrah was a burly, stately dog. His chest was exceptionally deep and served to lower his center of gravity between his stout forelegs. His tail, which hung stiffly between his buttocks, was encrusted with thistles and burrs and rather resembled a bailiff's cudgel. If Sirrah was conscious of the disheveled aspect of his appearance, he gave no outward sign, but kept his yellow eyes affixed to me, cataloging (I could not help but think) my damp, pale countenance, my posture, which by its slackness revealed one who was unaccustomed to these heights and the rigors of an existence he had endured for so many unvarying seasons. Had I been erect, our encounter might well have proceeded differently, with a proper authority accruing to the man rather than to the dog, but on my elbow, like a Roman senator on his pleasure couch, my eyes were just on Sirrah's level, and I understood too well that he, dog, was in his element here and that I was the interloper.

"You will not pat my head?" After his initial, confident perusal, Sirrah's request betrayed a milder aspect, and I hastened my assurances. He was reluctant to take me at my word: "You Americans are the worst. You cannot encounter a dog, going about its lawful business, without stooping to paw at it. If you fondle me, sir, I will not be responsible for the consequences."

Again I gave my word.

He came nearer then, though not so near he couldn't retire at the first sign of unwanted attentions. He flopped down among the stones, but evidently had thistles in his breast fur, for he twitched from one side to the other, trying to find comfort and at last drew back on his haunches, where he resumed his cool inspection. "You'll make no shepherd in this country," he said. "You have the legs for the job, but you are overfond, I see, of meat and strong drink."

I flushed. I said something about having sheep in America. I fiddled with my tape recorder. Its dials, switches, and chromium finish that, yesterday, had seemed so *serious*, had a different message for me: Today they were smug, obstinate, useless.

"America will be flat, then? A soft kind of place?"

"No. Not all flat."

Sirrah had fight scars on his dark, striped nose and some gray hairs as well. He had the demeanor of an experienced dog, one at the height of his powers. Without further ado, we began the interview.

"My mother, Matilda," Sirrah began boldly, "was a thief. She was the chief servant and sole confidante of Ossian MacDowell, whose depredations outraged the countryside from Broughton to Biggar town. While yet a lad, MacDowell had made twin discoveries, one on the heels of the other. He discovered in himself a detestation of honest work and a delight in gold sovereigns. Ossian found no contradiction in this, but set out to learn how he could obtain the latter without necessity of the former. I suppose if Matilda had been less keen, Ossian MacDowell might have failed in his ambition. My mother was a black-and-white bitch and, unlike me, had a wide white ruff for a collar. Any night with sufficient moon that MacDowell could see Matilda's ruff as she scoured another man's paddocks for sheep—that night suited Ossian MacDowell well enough. Ossian's whispered "Hist!" was enough to set mother on her way, and Ossian would proceed straightaway to the paddock gate where, promptly, Mother would reappear with a score of young ewes, not even panting at their unexpected exertions. Mother, Ossian MacDowell bragged, selected only 'Good uns,' but this was, doubtless, exaggeration. Though Ossian might drive his captives all night, on turnpike and over moor, circumnavigating the sheriff's men, even passing through flocks of honest sheep, Matilda never faltered. For a time she fetched him more gold than an honest stockman could have earned by dint of the severest labor, and she (and I, too) dined on fresh-killed meat and slept on clean straw in the box of Ossian's pony cart. In the pubs, we would settle under Ossian's bench while he entertained others no better than he. Ossian made up new verses to familiar tunes, oft times another would take up fiddle and bow and while the gay airs played, my mother would dance on her hinder legs—quite charming she was—and sometimes I'd sing.

His drinking mates warned Ossian that his activities were suspected, farmers who'd lost sheep kept secret watch on him day and night, but as long as he and Matilda could slip away onto the Hill, no man could catch them.

In the end, the butcher who bought from them betrayed them. Discovered with marked lambs in his yard, the butcher swore he'd been misled by that scoundrel Ossian MacDowell and 'that devil bitch of his.' "

Overcome by these recollections, Sirrah's voice faltered. "For his crimes, Ossian was transported to Botany Bay, but the convict camp couldn't hold him. Within a fortnight, he'd fled into the Australian hinterlands, where he resumed his sheep-stealing ways. Without Mother as accomplice, he fared poorly, was soon apprehended, and, on this occasion, hung. The Australian tune 'Waltzing Matilda' is, I understand, Ossian MacDowell's tribute to my mother."

Sirrah described the Broughton farmer who'd promptly murdered Ossian's bitch. She had, the farmer claimed, a thieving nature, and left alive, another thief would soon find the same employment for her Ossian MacDowell had. The farmer demanded the pup as partial recompense for his losses, and though Sirrah was a strong whelp, ready to start his life's work, the farmer hurled him into a dank windowless byre and left him to the attentions of the fleas and lice that inhabited that dark place.

"One afternoon," he continued, "the stone at the entrance of my tomb was rolled aside, and I was tugged into blinding sunlight. Whereupon, the farmer's son sold me to a cattle drover who hoped I would be useful, nipping the heels of cattle enroute to market. Thereafter, I marched behind muddy or dusty cattle from Peebles to Edinburgh, Galashiels to Lanark. Once his beasts were sold, and my master's purse engorged, he'd eye me with a thrifty, penny-pinching eye. My work was done. Should he abandon me to run with the packs of the similarly discarded curs who thronged these towns? Could he save a farthing by knocking me on the head? Fortunately, drink always interrupted these subtle calculations and always, next morning, I would once more be following behind him, attached to his cart by a rope as thick as my forepaw.

"When the drover was fu [drunk], it was his unvarying custom to lash me with this rope while inquiring in a bellow, 'What do you think about this, then, ye brute? How do ye ken this?' Whenever he returned to the cart, late, singing of Bonnie Dundee, I'd creep between the wheels and tremble.

"We were returning from Lanark market one spring morning, when I first encountered James Hogg. My master had squandered his droving fee on drink and a portion of the cattle price as well. Since those cattle had not been his own, this morning found him palsied, foul, and trembling, in short, of a mood to make any bargain.

"Oft times, Master Hogg has said he recognized my working abilities straightaway, the moment he looked at me, but I cannot swear to that. The guinea he bought me with was a full month's wages, and I took the place of the woolen cloak he badly required. I think he bought me of Christ's mercy."

The brute turned his head away then, that I mightn't remark the moisture welling in his great yellow eyes. When he continued, his deep voice was softer than it had been. "When that man bent to eye me in my eyes, I was more frightened than I'd been on those dark wild nights when I thought the drover meant to have my life. Though he was innocent of harm, Master Hogg would create something in me that hadn't been mine before. Looking into the eyes of James Hogg, that day, I felt the first painful stirrings of my soul."

Overcome by his recollections, he withdrew himself to a low outcropping, where he could peruse the harsh slopes of his eternal domain, and there he remained until he had recovered himself.

When he resumed his narrative, he began to pace before me, like a country schoolmaster exhorting his pupils to achieve a fine comprehension of matters that he, in the deepest recesses of his own heart, finds quite as puzzling as do his charges. "Some years after I first came to this place, I was given to understand that the drover who'd so abused me was due to arrive in his turn. All arrivals here, lowly and holy, appear at the Great Gates where they are welcomed. Our Lord dearly loves bazaars and marketplaces, and the Great Gates, I am told, are not unlike Jerusalem Market, though greater in scale. Here enter men and women and infants, christened though yet unable to walk (the angels gather these new souls to their bosoms, and I won't say who is gladdest, the angels or the burdens they joyfully endure). There are hostlers to meet arriving horses: *vaqueros, gauchos,* Comanches; how they elbow each other when some splendid steed comes through the gate. There are dog men for the dogs. And for the rare cats and tamed wild animals and pet zebus and ostriches and sheep, there are angels to explain things. I do not envy those angels—guiding, patiently counseling, allaying fears, but angels are ferlies, inexhaustible. It is a rare Babylon of languages, and with my own ears, I have heard an angel greeting a Sisserou Parrot in his own chittering tongue.

"Below the Great Gates, on a vast plain, wait those who have special interest in the day's arrivals, as well as the idly curious. Many a time, in the years after

Master Hogg arrived, he and I would wait there to greet old friends as they passed through the portals, but afore long, no more came whom he had known; costume became subtly altered, even speech. It is unusual for us to attend the Great Gates today. Master Hogg resides in Edinburgh and I, here." He took a draught of cold air, "On the Hill."

He left off his pacing and faced me directly. "Last spring, I was on an errand near the Great Gates and thought to see what manner of curiosities were coming through that day. Perhaps there'd been a war. What appeared, in a steady stream were thousands of short-haired brown-and-black dogs, long-eared feckless creatures, no brains at all, but sensitive noses and singing voices I envied. They were named "Blue Tick" and "Red Tick" and "Walker"—these were dogs that had hunted raccoons. Their arrival en masse, was prompted by a religious revival in the American district of Tennessee, where hundreds of men had been Saved [you call it 'Born Again'] and had forsworn all beer, ale and spirits and dispatched these dogs who'd been bred for entertainment these new Christians now thought dissolute."

Though he awaited my explanation politely, I didn't have one ready. I said I'd had neighbors who found Jesus, quit drinking Old Milwaukee Beer, sent their coon dogs to the pound, and washed their cars. In America, I said, there's a direct correlation between the strength of religious belief and how frequently you wash your car. But for my purposes, this was a digression. I asked what had happened when Sirrah's old Master, the drover, had come through the gates.

"Oh, aye. Him. I waited near the Great Gates, in the place allotted to those who've come to testify. I'd begged Master Hogg to shun the proceedings, since I had no desire to remind him of the sufferings I'd undergone. I had taken care with my grooming, and my black coat shone. Two of the drover's children had pre-

ceded me to the place, and there were other dogs waiting, too. One, a gray Dalesman, named Alf, I befriended
at once, and we had good crack about roads we'd traveled, market dogs we'd known. Three of the drover's
horses were there, too, though they were quite frightened and required repeated reassurance from the
Archangel that nothing ill would befall them by virtue
of their testimony. From what all said, there were
many other animals who might have wished to testify
today, but hadn't been given souls and so, on their
death, had been recombined. Standing apart from our
group was a small white mongrel terrier with a black
head and saddle. "Sonsie" announced she was a King
Charles Spaniel of regal descent and she'd come to
greet her beloved Master. Though she was no more
spaniel than I, she spoke so winsomely and gave herself such silly airs that we were more amused than
annoyed. 'Aren't I the pretty bitch?' she asked. 'Oh,
when I grew frail and elderly, I was no bonny then, but
when I first arrived here' (she clapped paws together)
'do you know what they asked me, first thing? They
asked me what age I wished to be, and I said, "My
heart is young!" Those were my very words and, oh!
My dreams came true.'

"The gray Dalesman and I concealed our smiles.

"We are not allowed to remember our passages:
Our birth and death are forever blank. The drover was
taken suddenly, kicked by a horse, in the course of his
ordinary business. Though the drover's hair was white
as the January snows, he was no frail, elderly gentle-
man, but vigorous, still harsh: a man with leather fists
and boots for those unwary enough to lie in his path.
The very moment he saw me, he launched a vicious
kick that, had it landed, would have discommoded me
for weeks. I am gratified to say he missed, clean, and
more gratified to recall the prompt revenge I took on
his ankle and thigh." Sirrah permitted himself a reminiscent smile.

"Then we testified. The issue is grave, and whenever any creature's fate is weighed in the balance, the poor soul waits at the Gates while those who knew him best testify as to character and habits. Sonsie, the wee white bitch, lavished praise. From her evidence, she had found the one soft recess in the drover's obdurate heart and insinuated herself there. Even as she spoke of his kindnesses to her, a smile flickered over the man's face—a smile that on any other face would be called gentle. It had been the drover who told Sonsie of her royal forebears, and I don't doubt they both believed the lie. As she babbled, she set herself beside his fierce boots, protecting him from all the world's opinions.

"The Archangel listened as we told our tales. The children spoke of neglect, blows, desperate filthiness. The boy had lost his life to the brute. The horses related sufferings that brought tears to the flintiest eye. And while we made the case against him, Sonsie bared her wee teeth and growled her wee growl."

Sirrah's expression was solemn as a magistrate's. "Our testimony was credited," Sirrah said shortly. "The abused carried the day."

"And so?"

"He went to a place where he can drink all he wishes." Sirrah paused. "The white dog chose to accompany him." He looked about for distraction and he attended to the thistles in his tail. His teeth clicked and clattered, and he soon had a thistle ball, intertwined with such of his own fur as he'd been unable to separate. Delicate as a Greek spitting pistachio hulls, he spat this ball aside.

Far below, Sirrah's apprentice, the younger dog, was pressing a stream of sheep across a broad headland that quit abruptly in a near vertical incline. Although a shepherd's instructions were urgent and audible to us, much farther above, the young dog was heedless. Sirrah cocked his head critically, "If Hector takes them that way, the ewes will balk."

And an instant later, as if sensible of the danger, the sheep began to swirl. Sirrah went to his vantage place and stretched to his full height. "We are each allowed only so much wisdom," he said. "And that whelp's allowed less than most. He has fetched the sheep off this hill so often I could not count the times; yet, each time, he tries to bring them where sensible sheep will not go." Realizing his mistake, the younger dog came around and gathered his charges to a less precipitous decline which, mollified, they entered gladly enough.

He wasn't taking the shepherd's commands, I noted.

"I misdoubt we have a shepherd today," Sirrah replied. Apparently he wished to be away after the sheep himself, and his clumsy tail twitched. "Master Hogg prefers pretty Edinburgh to the Hill and we oft must make do with his ferlie."

At the base of Broad Law, not far from where I'd begun my own ascent, I made out a man's figure, crook in hand, uttering sharp whistles, gruff commands. "A ferlie shepherd?"

"Aye. He looks like Master Hogg, whistles the Master's whistles, sleeps in the Master's loft in the byre." Angrily, he bit at his tail and at this time, spat out more hair than thistle. Although I itched to help him, and have extracted countless burrs from the tails of numerous dogs, I knew my attentions would be unwelcome.

Sirrah sighed. "Heaven would not be heaven for Master Hogg if he couldn't be in town with Walter Scott and the writing gentlemen, and heaven would be no heaven for me if I couldn't be on the hills working yon sheep. So, when needs be, Hector and I are supplied a ferlie shepherd. Naught, even heaven, is perfect."

"If they look the same and act the same, how do you know it's a ferlie?"

The look Sirrah gave me was too cold. "The Lord God is the God of Light," he said. "Not the God of Scent."

I had hoped to meet James Hogg, I said. He was a writer I much admired. Viv Billingham, I said, was another fan, and she was a very fine dog handler. I told Sirrah about Holly.

Sirrah lifted a single black forepaw and inspected it critically. "Master Hogg was a dab hand as a shepherd," he said. "He was hard pressed to earn stale oatcakes for me when I had need of such nourishment, and when he tenanted his own farm, things grew worse. In April, when agriculturalists are sowing their crops, Master Hogg would be crowded against the peat fire, scribbling verses. When the lambs were dropping on the hill, sometimes he'd be assisting, but more often he'd be away with the literary gentlemen. Oh, the gentlemen greatly admired Master Hogg's tales of the shepherding he should have been attending to whilst he was describing it so particularly, snug in their admiration, a pint in his paw. He did some rare shepherding in Edinburgh town."

The ferlie shepherd blew sharp, insistent commands and Hector, the young dog stopped in his tracks, looked back up the hill he'd so recently quitted and clambered a second time to gather a band of sheep that had been concealed by the uneven terrain.

A cloud interposed itself between us and the sun. A deep chill attended its shadow's passage across the face of the hill. I tugged my jacket across my chest. "I suppose a ferlie shepherd is better than none," I said.

"None of us have all the heaven we want. Only poor deluded creatures are perfectly happy, and the Lord permits no delusions in His Home." Sadness overtook his countenance. "When I first came, I auditioned for the heavenly choirs. I've always loved the grand Covenanter hymns, and it was my hope to sing daily, praising His works, lauding His works and ways. The choral masters heard me courteously, but advanced the suggestion that my singing might, perhaps, be more appropriate to a more rural setting. Although my songs were acceptable to the Lord, other singers found them infelicitous. They replaced me with a Blue Tick hound and two Welshmen.

I shivered. "It feels like snow."

He brightened, lifted his snout into the wind. "I have seen snow on these heights in August," he said.

I was surprised there'd be such weather here. "I thought it would be more comfortable."

He grinned his doggy grin. "It can get bitter on these heights, and the winds, how they blow. And a February storm on Broad Law can try the mettle of dog and shepherd alike. There's been many a roaring night Hector and I have thought we would perish on this Hill, but, of course, how could we?" He barked a laugh. "What comfort is the hearth fire without raw weather howling outside the door, and what pleasure is there in rest unless the day's toil was almost more than you could bear? Oh, we are often wet, frozen, miserable, and the ice rimes our fur, but we are given strength to bear it. . . ."

After a pause, I inquired, "So you work these hills, year round, with a ferlie shepherd?"

When he stretched himself, the strong muscles corded his back.

"James Hogg wrote well about you," I tried another tack.

"I suppose that's sufficient? He sold me! Aye, selling a dog like myself; that's an ill thing. But to write about it, to publish your regrets for the world to read and to sell those regrets to put a crust of bread on your table, Christ!" He ripped again at his tail and deposited a clot of nasty material on the earth beside him. When he heard the scratching of my writing instrument, he winced and corrected himself scrupulously.

"If Master Hogg had not feared for his own employment (for such were his circumstances when he sold me), he would have kept me at his side." He paused. "He does come back, you know. To Broad Law. In the spring, with Edinburgh friends. Oh, I am devilish excited then. Sometimes I sing like a pup. The literary gentlemen take short walks along the softer paths, admire the vistas and flowers, and soon retire to the cottage with their pipes and whiskey, where they discuss the proper uses of the Scottish language and those poems presently fashionable in the French salons. They will have new stories—every spring, a dozen new stories they recite to one another. And Hector and I lie at James Hogg's feet, and the literary talk falls across our backs like crumbs from the table. . . ." He rose to his feet and paced restlessly. "Once, oh it was three or four seasons past, Master Hogg returned to the Hill. It was September—just this time of year. He told me he'd tired of town life, that the town was false and malicious. He'd had work rejected by his publisher, and, I gather, a tale of his caused offense to personages he daren't offend. He remained here for three weeks and a day. It was grand."

Below us, the clouds lay in a thick woolly mat, and I fancied I could sense bad weather en route. "You say you've had blizzards in August?"

The shepherd had vanished and mists concealed the summits of Black Law and Dollar Law. I stood to stamp circulation into my feet. I rubbed my hands together and yearned for dry socks. "So, Edinburgh's heaven for poets, and the hill is heaven for you. 'In my Father's house there are many mansions', I suppose."

He eyed me strangely. I was out of order, like a sheep that wanders off the track without reason.

"And there are other heavens than this hill, I persisted. "Tropical heavens, monastic heavens, heavens where the Born Again can wash their cars . . ."

Sirrah's tongue lolled out. "They'll be dipping the sheep afore noon," he said. "Hector is no use at the pens. . . ."

"And where is your mother?"

"I am told Matilda is in the Outback of Australia. I fear for the security of the sheep flocks there."

"With Ossian MacDowell?"

"Just so." The cold sun lit up hair on his spine, and I fancied I saw glints of dark, dark red. I sat again, tucking my knees to my chest. He'd been anticipating the interview's end and mocked me by sitting himself, with an ancient's groan. The cloud ocean was climbing our slope. "Which were your greatest storms?" I asked.

He furrowed his brow. "We've had so many," he spoke slowly, "and each comes upon us afresh, as if it never had a predecessor." More happily, he said, "When the sheep are buried in the drifts, it's Hector who digs them out. I've never known a better dog for it. When I ask him how he locates them, sometimes under yards of crusted snow, he tells me 'You could do it, too, auld man, if you had a lighter spirit.' Daft!" His doggy brow wrinkled, and in a bit, he said, "It is a curious truth that I cannot remember the snows here in any particular. When I am in my straw bed at night, it is not these storms that I dream about, but always, springtimes and storms below. In my dreams, I forget my century in heaven and recall only my few springtimes on earth." Rousing himself from revery, he started and glared at me. "You write down that I have the greatest appreciation of Master Hogg's merits," he said. And he watched as my instrument inscribed his dictation. "I don't know that I have been happier since I met Master Hogg, but it was he who gave me my soul."

I coughed. "Just so."

"Do you think he wished to do it? Do any of you? Must we beasts pray for your mercies?" He was suddenly angry, and I pulled my feet close until he calmed.

"I suppose you cannot help yourselves, it is how you are made. You men boast of your works, machines, poems, warrior skills: ape chatter. Why do you think the tenderest of God's sweet creatures love you? Poor babies, you give us souls." Sirrah's left ear flicked upright. "Do you hear that, Man?"

I looked up from my scribblings, rather dazed. Hear what?

He strained. He poured his whole self into his hearing, in vain. Nervously, he went on. "I was born a sheepdog. Had I been born a singer, I would praise God with my songs. If I were a thoroughbred hunter, I would soar over hedges and fences for Him. Somewhere, here, coon dogs are praising God with their marvelous tongues, though I'm afraid their hunters will all be ferlie ones—Hark to that, Man! I know that whistle!"

If I'd known it was going to get this cold, I would have worn a thicker jersey. It had taken me the better part of two hours to climb here. I prayed going down would be quicker. I didn't care for the look of those clouds. A wet, fat, snowflake smacked into my cheek.

"Oh Man, can you not hear it? That wee flourish at the tail of the whistle, that pretty trill?"

Rather stuffily I said, "Sorry, no. Your ears are so much better than mine." I worried that flying snow would soon make my notebook as useless as my recorder had proved to be. Though Sirrah was extremely agitated, raising up on his hind legs to hear better, he did respond to my questions as quickly as I asked them. Where was he born?

"Biggar. Horse stable beside the high road."

Place of death?

"Ettrick. They were kind to me. The old man cushioned my head in his lap." Sirrah's body began to shake. "That's Master Hogg's whistle. I cannot mistake it. Oh, James loves Broad Law in the fall, when the heather is blooming. He'll take a wee sprig of white heather and fix it to his lapel and walk the footpaths, dreaming his poetry."

"Not the ferlie shepherd's whistles?"

"Ach, man! The ferlie but *mocks* Master Hogg! Nay, it is him. I'd know James Hogg's whistles anywhere!"

"You've said you praise God by your work. How does that differ from what you did on Earth?"

"Master Hogg is home!" he cried and hurled himself off the heights toward that, to me, inaudible summons, at a breakneck pace, bounding from ledge to ledge like a mountain goat. In seconds, his dark muscular shape was swallowed up by the rolling clouds.

A snowflake splashed my page, and that smudge is the only proof of Sirrah I retain today.

Without the dog's guidance, mine was a cold, cautious, nasty descent. All the universe beyond what lay beneath my feet was blanked out by the mists. I don't recall how I found my way down, and, safe on the earth again, when I looked up at the underside of the clouds, I saw nothing I hadn't seen before.

6

The Bonny Wee Bitch

On Eye Exam Tuesday, I wore gray work pants and a flannel shirt. I had a collar for the wee bitch and a lead. I'd bought a dog bowl and some dog food. I dearly hoped Gael wasn't cow hocked or parrot mouthed or cross-eyed useless. I prayed I'd seen what I thought I'd seen. Tuesday was bright, quite nice. I had difficulty finding Tom Reid's turnoff, though I'd found it before, at night, half drunk, without the slightest difficulty. I was delaying, afraid of what I might find there.

A chipper Tom Reid meets me at the door and says, "I would offer ye a wee dram, but I canna. Some of the lads came by last night."

Reid is dressed in fresh suit, cap, and tie. He has his ISDS badge in the lapel, and his handkerchief is folded neatly in his breast pocket. He has, he says, phoned David McTeir, and Mister McTeir understood. Perhaps McTeir'll come over and see the other three-year-old bitch. "I'll have to have twelve hundred for her." Perhaps the American would like to see her go?

"Sure."

We drive back to the same field I'd seen only once before, at dusk. The same tups huddle against the same far fence. A pretty place to train a dog. Reid steps over the wire fence and sets his three-year-old bitch loose. She is a hearty thing, heavy, squat, and very excitable. "I've only had her mesel a fortnight."

The bitch cuts in too close to the sheep and gets a mouthful of wool. When she finally does lie down, she sticks and doesn't want to get up again. After her slight exertion, she pants like a blown horse. I say (politely) that she's going well for only a fortnight's training and Reid will soon put her right. I note she'd have difficulties in the States where it's so much hotter.

"Aye," Reid sighs, "Weel. . . ."

I am sorry Reid doesn't have a second good bitch but, at the same time, feel relief. If I can spot the flaws in *this* bitch, maybe I wasn't foolish about the wee one. "We should be going," I say. "It's a fair bit to Glasgow."

In the full light of day, Gael's neither parrot mouthed nor cow hocked and has limpid lemur eyes. She's built like a whippet, muscle stretched taut over bone. One ear points forward, the other's half-cocked to the rear. She's black and tan except for her white breast, a neck ring silly as a cheap boa, and white forelegs like long kidskin gloves drawn to her elbow. She reminds me of Rona, a Jewish girlfriend of my New York days; Gael has the same deep Mediterranean eyes.

Reid jumps both bitches into the boot of my car.

The old herd directs me to all the slow roads, winding through villages, pointing out farms and people he's known all his life. Once a month he'd drive his wife north, to Glasgow, for the cancer treatments. "She was niver sick," he says, "Niver had a sick day in her life."

He'd been a shepherd in the hills above Girvan. It was a hungry house. He and the other workers would take meals in the farmhouse kitchen, skim milk on their porridge, while the farmer's family ate in the dining room, taking all the cream. He worked there through the sixties, shepherding that high lonely ground, him and his dogs.

Tom Reid's first dog was Jim. Tom was eight years old when his father sold Jim. "I hate to sell a dog," Tom says. "I dinna like it."

Farmer's lung impairs his circulation, which is how he lost his leg. The hospital was all right except for the telly. Other patients watched the football games all the time, but he doesn't care for football. His good leg gets stiff traveling, and he rubs it from time to time.

He had Gael's mother put to MacKenzie's Don. "They say Don didn't breed well, but when he did, it was a topper." Since Don's owner, Perry MacKenzie, lives in Caithness, in the north, after Don won the International, the dog was boarded south with the Shennans, where more bitches were available. Reid thinks perhaps seventy bitches were put to Don. He laughs. "I wouldna have put my bitch to him if I'd known what an ugly brute Don was."

I got lost in Glasgow. Tom Reid was ill at ease in the city and not pleased to be lost. "I couldna live here," he asserted. "I wouldna."

He'd come to Carswilloch to retire. He had his bit from the government. Now and then he'd help with the tups. He'd always been a great one for the tups.

We found the veterinary college and ate lunch at an Indian restaurant. Reid said he didn't like Indian food; he liked honest British fare like gammon, chips, and curry. He was allergic to corn, rice, and wheat. The tinted eyeglasses shaded his cataracts.

Both bitches passed their test, eyes fine. Pupils dilated, blind, Gael got in the car when Reid asked her to. "You canna abuse a dog," he said softly. "They never forget it. Until their dying day they willna forget it was you abused them."

As the cooler shadows lengthened, we drove back south.

It was just this time of day that Reid had his car smashup. He and his wife returned from Glasgow, after her cancer treatment, and badly wanted some fresh air, so they took Gael out. As always, quietly, Gael rode between his wife's feet. It's a long clear stretch of road before the Carswilloch turn, and Tom slowed, as he had hundreds of times, and touched his indicators and turned. The lorry behind them was coming very quick, had slowed not a whit, and WHUMP they hurled sideways down the road. It was Tom's door that got crushed, pressed around his sound right leg, and his first thought was, "Dear God, not the other one." His wife was white faced and making some cry, he wasn't sure what, and she had her door open and was out on the tarmac. She wasn't hurt that he could see, but she wasn't in her right mind either and Tom took hold of the wee bitch's collar before she could escape the car because she was a wild thing and once she was out, she was away. The wee bitch did her terrified best, used teeth and claw in her urgency. "Bide there, Lass. Bide there, Lass. Bide there. . . ."

At the cottage, he took my money and gave me ten pounds back for luck. I promised to write. I said, "I'll be back for the International. Maybe I'll see you then."

"Aye," Reid said. "If I'm spairt."

And I took Tom Reid's bonny wee bitch away.

When I fastened Gael's lead to the passenger door latch, she was frightened and squirmed over the transmission hump under my feet and she couldn't ride there, it was too dangerous, so I shifted my luggage to the trunk and overturned the clamshell kennel in the backseat and she scooted under its shelter, gratefully. That's how we traveled: me in the front, her in the back, shedding her coat all over the rental car's passenger compartment.

I'd changed categories again. I'd been a man with a desire: now I was a man with a companion. That night, I stayed at Windy Hill Farm outside Strathaven, where my hostess was quite taken with Gael. "She's a fetching little thing." That night Gael slept in the kennel and first thing in the morning I got down and knelt beside it to be sure she hadn't evaporated in the night.

A lifetime ago, on my first day in Britain, a tabloid newspaper reported the sad loss of a London Border Collie who'd habitually waited at the subway stop to greet his master home from work. A neighborhood newcomer thought the dog was a stray, took him around to the police who failed to identify him, turned him over to the animal shelter and by the time the owner finally tracked the dog down, all that was left was the collar. The constable who'd failed to identify the dog was deeply distressed, the family was furious, and the newcomer was disparaged as a busybody.

The story was on page one. It wouldn't have been news in the States. After we discount the tabloid's lust for sentimentality, there is a residue: Presumptions made in Britain and America about the nature of dogs are so different, the two cultures might be describing distinct taxonomical species.

Canis Familiarus Britannicus is a well-mannered beast you can take anywhere: on trains, subways (if he's little enough to tote on the escalators), on buses and quietly under the table at the pub while his master has a wee dram.

Canis Familiarus Americanus is a willful but CUTE creature who cannot be trusted in modern civilization.

In *Hondo*, an early John Wayne western, Wayne plays a cavalry scout who slips through hostile Indian territory accompanied only by his faithful (collie?)

Sam. When Wayne arrives at the Lonely Widow's homestead and she attempts to feed Sam, Wayne chides her, says that Sam hunts his own food. "Sam's independent. It's better that way."

In *Harper's* magazine, recently, Ingrid Newkirk, National Director of PETA (People for the Ethical Treatment of Animals) described the dog's fate in a society that embraced animal rights: "For one thing, we would no longer allow breeding. People could not create different breeds. . . . If people had companion animals in their homes, those animals would have to be refugees from the animal shelters and the streets. You would have a protective relationship with them, just as you would with an orphaned child. But as the surplus . . . declined, eventually companion animals would be phased out, and we would return to a more symbiotic relationship—enjoyment at a distance."

Besides their ignorance of dogs, the John Wayne character and Ms. Newkirk share a curious contempt for them. Those poor, stupid, pampered creatures—wouldn't they be better off wild?

It has been twenty thousand years since man and dog formed their partnership. That we have altered the dog genetically is well understood; it is hardly known how they changed us. Since dogs could hear and smell better than men, we could concentrate on sight. Since courage is commonplace in dogs, men's adrenal glands could shrink. Dogs, by making us more efficient predators, gave us time to think. In short, dogs civilized us.

"The wild" has always had a grip on the American psyche. "In wilderness," Henry David Thoreau said, "is the salvation of the world." Only an American could say that and only an American could think it self-evidently true. "Wild" animals are animals unscrewed up by man or, in a different mood, creatures we can slaughter to our heart's content. Wilderness is the place where the centuries-old limits on human conduct no longer apply, where a man is a *man* and a dog is a wolf.

My home county is rural and my neighbors let their dogs run free, returning home for meals and sleep. These dogs are killed by cars, dispatched by farmers who catch them attacking their sheep, slain by hunters who see them running deer. Most simply vanish.

When I suggest my neighbors might adopt some other strategy of dog care, they look at me like I'm crazy: Don't I know a dog wants to roam, wants to be as wild as it can be?

In America, dogs are rarely seen in offices, shops, subways, trains or buses, and only in our mountain West will you find a dog in a bar. Sometimes I think Americans are afraid of dogs.

Britain is a country where limits are real, limits of birth and geography. Although portions of the island are remote and rugged, these areas are protected as "parks," not "wilderness." The downside of British limits is obvious: It would have been much easier for the Billinghams to become entrepreneurs in America. But the nature of dog training is limits—the dog has his, the sheep have theirs and, most important, the man has limits too. To go beyond those limits, to force the training, to ask the dog to understand what is beyond him invites failure. Working within and against their limits, a flawed man and flawed dog can sometimes achieve a kind of elegance that looks very much like perfection.

I drove Gael to Tweedhope right away. I wanted the confirmation of eyes more skilled than my own.

Viv said, "The wee bitch looks just like you, Donald. All gingery." Fearing she'd offended, she added, "I think Garry looks just like me. Can't you see it?"

I fancied I saw a resemblance.

Viv, Geoff, and I took Gael out to the bluff overlooking the glen where the tups grazed—the tups Viv used for her dog demonstrations. They grazed contentedly on an island surrounded by shallow burns.

"Shall I send Holly to bring them near?" Viv asked.

"Let's see what Gael can do," I said and unfastened the lead and stood her beside my leg and sent her off with a "whssst," and she was away, down the bluff, wading/swimming the burn, up nicely behind the tups, and they faced her, a stubborn wall of wool, hooves, and bone.

"Call her on, Donald."

"Let's see what she does by herself." Gael came on softly, deliberately, until the tups had enough and turned and splashed into the burn. Once she had the tups heading nicely, she swung back to collect an unfortunate goat lingering nearby. The goat knew she wasn't part of this act and kept trying to bolt. Gael balanced nicely—the three cheeky tups and the flighty, desperate goat—and brought all four through the burn to the foot of the bluff. Gael was hard to call off, she was so happy.

"She's brilliant, Donald," Viv said. "Brilliant."

Geoff, more quietly: "Aye. Yin's a useful bitch."

That night, in Peebles, most of the B & Bs were full up but I found a room, finally, in a house with just one room to rent, at the top of the stairs. The owner, a pleasant young man, was a builder by trade, and his house wasn't quite finished: a heap of lumber beside the front door, a cinderblock serving for the front stoop. The Edinburgh commuters (he said) were driving the house prices up; this place was worth twenty thousand more than he'd paid for it.

Under the eaves, my room was lit by brand-new clerestory windows. It'd be hot up here in the summertime, but it was nice enough now. The bathtub was surrounded by kids' bathtub toys. I lay on the thick featherbed, reading Bobby Burns, and the bonny wee bitch jumped up, like she'd been on featherbeds all her life, and started cleaning her feet. She made me smile. That night she slept beside me, her hard boney back pressed against my broader one.

Monie a sair darg we twa hae wrought,
An wi the weary warl' fought!
An monie an anxious day, I thought,
We wad be beat!
Yet here to crazy age we're brought,
Wi something yet.

In the morning, I drove north again. I wanted to see Gael's sire to learn, if I could, what genetic blessings and headaches lurked within her modest frame. As we neared Edinburgh, we joined the morning rush hour—thick, exhaust fumes, slow. I never got used to the pure open countryside surrounding the Scottish cities. This side of the bridge: verdant farmland. That side: habitations, wall to wall, thick as cliff dwellings.

Edinburgh streets are narrow, and cars were parked on both sides. When I spotted the laundrette, I also spotted an open parking space just across the street. I zipped into the space and waited for a break in traffic before opening my door and . . .

Gael jumped into the street.

"GAEL." I didn't shout, but my alarm sped directly to her brain stem and when her four feet hit the tarmac, she landed like a lunar lander: stopped, on the spot where she'd put down. "Gael, that'll do, here," and she scampered back inside the car and a baker's lorry whooshed by and I closed the car door so it wouldn't get ripped off. I couldn't remember if I'd taken my blood-pressure pills.

That's what loss is; how quick it happens.

Gael hated the car, despised the curvy single track roads, loathed the motorways with their hurry-up noise and vibration.

In the central Highlands we stopped for lunch in Blair Atholl Village. It was a smallish place and the hills lifted sharply from the valley. I wondered where they'd hold the International—somewhere on Blair Castle's grounds, I'd been told. I'd pretty well decided to come back in September for the big trial. Having got to know the dogs at the beginning of the season, I hoped to see them at the finish, polished and superb.

We got back on the motorway and headed north.

Inverness is crooked streets, difficult traffic, annoying. In Inverness, a busker (street musician) sits from early morning to dusk on the principal bridge across the River Ness. He plays the tin whistle. Some buskers are accomplished musicians. This one plays the same four notes over and over. In the morning, he plays his monody slowly, in the afternoon rapidly. Doubtless he is to be pitied, doubtless he is mad, but his seems a singularly Inverness way to make a living: by irritation.

I found parking underneath a new shopping mall in the town center. The garage was dark and concrete and echoing, with not much room between car bumpers, and Gael kept tight to my side. The exit doors were marked in red stencil: Emergency Exit Only, so I followed arrows into the building itself, where it was much quieter, and the floor was linoleum (cream colored), and the sign on the single door said: Please, No Dogs.

Stateside malls have such signs, and I wondered if the sign had come across the water with the mall concept.

I wondered what the mall's owners thought Gael was going to do. Perhaps her fault was being an animal, on the premises, with no intention to buy.

Of course, it might have just been Inverness. I strode through the door and, a guard buttonholed me, "Sorry sir, no dogs allowed" and I didn't even pause because I saw a way out forty feet away, "I'm just leaving thanks," and gone, got away with it.

That night I stopped at a B & B in Dingwall, in the north. Once more, mine was the only rental room, and the mother shushed the kids for fear they'd wake the American when they ran up the stairs.

Above Lairg, along Loch Shin, is where they had the last Clearances, a hundred years ago. In some parishes, a thousand crofters were evicted in a single day. This was a hard land, the hardest I'd seen in Scotland. Even the gorse bushes seemed appealing—most other vegetation was peat moss and lichen. It reminded me of stretches of the American West. The streams ran silver beside the road, and it wasn't country I'd like to break down in at night.

Scottish National Radio interviewed a professor of folk culture who'd gotten his start when Alan Lomax came over in the thirties. Lomax wanted to collect folk ballads of the Highlands and the Isles, and fifty years ago this professor was his guide.

The fish lorries came very fast, wouldn't back down, and twice almost ran me off the road. Just beyond the hamlet of Badcall (a name that belongs in Montana) is an adventure school, its earnest youngsters training to be self-reliant, learning skills for a world that once existed in fact, but now exists only as sport. Stringent fitness is much more appealing when the society no longer needs it.

Adventure schools have their own ecological requirements, and the presence of one describes the local terrain. Here, along the empty shore, the road weaves between boulders the size of caravans. This is a moonscape, littered by meteorites. Here and there, there's a smidgen of browse for livestock.

J. P. (Perry) MacKenzie has the caravan park at Old Shore, beyond the modern fishing port of Kinlochbervie. The instant I let Gael out, Don, her father, hurries over (he *is* an ugly brute) and sniffs her in a businesslike way. He expects only one sort of bitch to visit him and wants to get on with it. For a moment, Gael trots along, ignoring the presumptuous stranger, until she turns and shows Don every tooth in her head. Gael has more teeth than a crocodile.

Perry MacKenzie is a ruddy-faced man with a double chin and a proprietor's manner. His handshake is brusque. "What sort of dogs de ye prefer?" he asks, right off.

I mutter something about dogs that think for themselves. I have no use, I say, for dogs that need commanding all the time.

Perry MacKenzie's nod means I'm over the first hurdle. "Won't ye come in? The wife has fixed tea."

We stand, rather awkwardly, in Mrs. MacKenzie's tidy parlor while she sets the dining-room table. Perry MacKenzie needs no prompting to launch into an account of Don's greatest trials. Though Perry doesn't really have words to describe those moments, clearly he sees them himself: "Steady Don," Perry says, crouched beside the settee, his hand guiding his envisioned dog around the handler's post, "Steady, Lad. . . ." Then, at the shedding ring there's this one ewe, frightened, she pushes herself in amongst the others, buries herself and she's the one they must have. Perry MacKenzie takes a step past the end table, points, "This yin!" And, damned if I don't see it too, as Don flashes in, a blur of black and tan, and singles the ewe.

We have cold gammon and a salad, which contains bananas, tomatoes, raisins, and lettuce. So far north, I cannot think where they've found this produce. The salad is in my honor. Scots don't care for them.

When John Angus MacLeod first saw MacKenzie's Don, he told Perry Don would have a fair shot at the International, but it'd be hellish to get him qualified. Don had worked the great empty hills behind Old Shore; smaller trial courses would be difficult for such a wide-running dog.

After tea, a genial Perry MacKenzie takes Don out. His ewes are on the Hill (six thousand acres of tundra), but he's got tups near. Don flashes out over the paddocks and fetches them into a small fenced lot.

The bright blue sky, the pale northern sun: It's cold here in the early afternoon. Don and his son, Vick, push the sheep from one side, Gael presses them from the other. Perry compresses his tups like a man compressing a spring. "Get up Lassie, get up." And the wee bitch steps near, nearer, and the tups are head down, pawing, ready to charge. Gael is well inside the line where they'll fight her.

"Don't you think that's good enough?" I ask.

"Get up, Lass. Nothing to worry about. No MacKenzie's Don bitch ever gripped a sheep."

I don't give a damn for the sheep. Those huge tups could flatten the wee bitch into a welcome mat. Gael takes MacKenzie's commands gladly. She's ready for stronger direction than I can give her.

And that's how grown men and fine dogs spend a few hours, shifting reluctant sheep here and there under the subarctic sun. When I say I must be going, Perry MacKenzie says I could leave the wee bitch if I wished to and laughs and says what a great pleasure it has been.

That night, I stopped in the fishing village of Helmsdale. Helmsdale was quiet. Narrow cobbled streets, fishing docks. Down by the docks, I let Gael off lead so she could run around and sniff.

The elderly woman who owned the B & B took to Gael right away. "Oh, she thinks weel o' herself."

"She does."

Perhaps my bedroom had been her daughter's, perhaps her own before her husband died. There was no surface in the room without a souvenir plate or doily or knickknack. Gael jumped right onto the bed and plumped herself down.

The restaurant I found was unprepossessing but good. The seafood was fresh, cooked simply, and I had a glass of wine with my meal. It was in celebration. I hoped my wife would like Gael. Tomorrow, I'd turn my car south for London and the long flight to America.

My farm is in an Appalachian county that, like

Scotland, has fewer citizens than it once had. In 1900, the county's population was 5,400. There are fewer than 2,600 souls today. Those who left come home for the church homecomings and family reunions and the county fair and hunting season. "I'm kin to old Joe Lockridge, remember Joe?" "I grew up on the Hiner place, down on Muddy Run." Those who stayed in the county were the fortunate, the slightly prosperous, the stubborn, the less visionary, the eldest sons.

My ancestors left Scottish shores how many generations ago? Perhaps they stood with Charlie at Culloden. Perhaps they resisted Charlie's call but were sold out by their own chieftains during the Clearances.

The McCaigs left the Highlands not because they wanted to, but because they were starving. And when they went to Glasgow or Edinburgh, they starved there, too. Their sins were being born poor, being unlucky.

Immigration is sadness on both sides of the ocean.

Gael was the immigrant now. I hoped she'd like her new home, new purposes, new climate.

I walked slowly back through Helmsdale's quiet streets.

When I opened the door to my room, the wee bitch was plopped on the middle of the bed with a toy sheep in her mouth. Just a scrap of wool, the toy had buttons for eyes. I put the red ribbon back around its damp neck and returned it to the dresser, where Gael had deftly extracted it from among the porcelain knicknacks.

When I pulled back the coverlet, the bonny wee bitch marched toward me and I flipped the coverlet at her and she batted it down. Again I flipped it, again she batted it. She was grinning. She pranced. When I got into bed, she dropped beside me and flipped onto her back and wriggled and said, "Arrrrr." I scratched her sweet pink belly. I wished I was a dog.

7

Pip's Welcome Home

It was getting dark when we clattered down the lane to our farmhouse. My wife, Anne, was driving. Gael lay quietly at my feet where she'd been since we left Dulles Airport.

As we unpacked the car, Pip came out to see what was going on but he didn't jump up or carry on or anything. He eyed me strangely and I think he was trying to figure out how long I'd been gone. He barked, once. He went over to make his acquaintance with the wee bitch.

The next morning, early, I took both dogs to the orchard for a walk. Except for a narrow path, the grass was quite tall and, suddenly, Pip shot off and vanished, ignoring my whistles and calls. Some dog handler, eh?

Annoyed, I continued along for ten minutes or so until I heard a low rumble, a drumming noise, and

over the rise came our sheep, all 120 of them and behind came Pip, balancing nicely. I don't know how he
found them, the grass was taller than his head.

I laid Gael down and told Pip, that'll do, here, and
he came readily to my feet. His tongue was lolling out
and he was grinning.

"You already got a good dog, Boss. What do we
need another dog for?"

8

John Angus
and the Buffalo

In September I returned to Scotland for the International. There was nobody waiting for me at Crainlarich. As the night sleeper from London pulled out, I was left alone on the platform, scrubbed dark by last night's rain. In Scotland, the distinction between public and private is not absolute, and someone had planted red and orange flowers in a wooden tub beside the Scotrail underpass. The roofs of Crainlarich village lay across the tracks, below.

Crainlarich is a popular terminus for hill walkers, but mid-September, when the heather is rust and lavender on the hills, is late for their vigorous enthusiasms.

A workman backed a repair engine onto a siding. An old man—he was lean enough to be a hill shepherd—trundled his bicycle into the underpass. He carried an oversized bindle (homeless?) perched across the handlebars.

Highland hills can be aloof and forbidding, but the slopes above the village were mild, almost feminine. The specks way up near the top—those were sheep.

The old man bumped his bicycle onto the platform and went back into the underpass for his bindle. "Good morning," I said. He kept his own counsel.

The station tearoom had a sign: No Rucksacks, Please! Inside, the walls were tongue and groove, and all the tables lined up side by side like a dining car. The poster of the huffing steam locomotive over the serving counter was for sale: two pounds. No, the scones weren't ready yet. Yes, I could have a cup of white coffee. The menu offered the breakfast special: sausage, eggs, bacon, toast, juice, and coffee, just one pound, ninety. Scotland has one of the higher heart disease rates in Europe.

I sat on my suitcase outside. A stocky young man hurried up the stairs and examined me with his working eye—the other was fish-belly white. "What time is it?"

I said. His clothes were fresh, but his skin was day-old.

"Eight in the morning or eight at night?"

"Morning."

"Oh, thank Jesus! Tell me, have you seen a bunch of navvies about? Workmen?"

I told him about the repair engine, but he didn't seem interested. He asked what day it was.

"Christ," he said. "The bastards gone off without me." He noted, "It was the drink," and disappeared down the stairs pursuing his job.

It was not so much longer before John Angus MacLeod arrived, shook my hand, and said, "Hello, Donald. Good to see you again." He complained that they'd moved the car park since last he'd come here and he'd returned home last night from the Grampian

Sheepdog Trials (the television trials) and raced to Blair Atholl to walk the big course, which was hellish. "Donald, the bloody thing is flat as a pancake."

The one-eyed man came up and said to me, "If I knew you were waiting for *him*, I'd have stayed talking to you longer."

John Angus's car is a Renault DS, a touring sedan, which passes the MOT (vehicle inspection) with luck. The car has electric windows and door locks and a five-speed transmission, and the elaborate tachometer is centered on the dash. Under feed sacks and tatty rain gear, the upholstery may be genuine broadcloth. The rear package shelf has been backwards hinged, in a manner its designers never anticipated, by dogs traveling in the boot (trunk), who, from time to time, push their heads up to get a look where they're going. The car smells, not unpleasantly, of pipe tobacco.

John Angus is uncomfortable with machines and drives poorly, lugging the big sedan up the grades, ignoring the tachometer.

Thirty-five years ago, the *London Daily Mail* sponsored a sheepdog trial in Hyde Park and invited John Angus and his pal, Raymond MacPherson, to compete. It's a forty-mile trek on a single-track road from Lochialort to Fort William, and slow around the flanks of Ben Nevis, past Glencoe and Loch Lomond into Glasgow. London lies south. In 1953, when the boys made their journey, the roads were worse. Since neither had a driver's license, they borrowed Raymond's father's.

John Angus MacLeod is a gaunt, long-armed, long-legged man in his mid-fifties. He has the highlander's great humped nose. His teeth are gapped on either side of his mouth, which is a convenience for his pipe. He's run at the International Sheepdog Trial thirteen or fourteen times, he can't remember. When I ask if any other Scot has run so many times, he doesn't remember that either, "Oh there's Johnny (John Templeton) and Raymond (Raymond MacPherson), I suppose."

John Angus came third at the Loughborough International with Glen, seventh with Ben at Armathwaite. Thus far this trial season, John Angus has taken four firsts, seven seconds, five thirds, two dozen fourths, fifths, and sixths. It's not been a season where any dog and handler have dominated the competition, and John Angus has done as well as anyone.

In June, when I was last in Scotland, sheepdog men would say to me, "Aye, ye'll have to meet John Angus." They'd always say this with a smile that was both deprecatory and admiring—a *Scottish* sly smile. Everyone had a story about John Angus—how he'd stopped an International to claim one of his sheep was blind. At another trial when he failed to pen his sheep, he'd explained, "There was a bee in the pen. That's why yin hellish ewe wouldn't go in." After one particularly poor showing, John Angus had gone to a drystane wall and banged his forehead against the stones until he bled.

With the dogs, he is dangerous.

Our road ran along the River Dochart, which was foaming brown. Scotland had had a rainy summer. I asked how he'd done in the Grampian Television Trials. "Aye, Taff won it," John Angus replied, shortly.

Taff—a five-year-old male—is John Angus's top trial dog. A burly, black-and-white, long-coated dog with a snout striped like a polecat's, Taff ran at the International with the English team in 1986, and last month John Angus qualified him to run in 1988 with the Scots. Taff goes back to Gilchrist Spot, who was an extraordinarily clever dog, but hardheaded. Ray Edwards, Taff's breeder and trainer, had hoped to come to Scotland for this International, but on account of the fall lamb sales, hadn't been able.

"How's Flint?" I asked, fearing I'd hear John Angus had sold him. When I last saw Flint, he and John Angus had had a falling out.

"The bugger's gone blind on me," John Angus said.

An International-caliber sheepdog handler needs

two first-rate dogs. The trial season runs from late April until September, and a keen handler might run four or six trials in a week. (Bobby Dalziel and his eminent Dryden Joe have won more than fifty trials.) Such trialing puts tremendous pressure on a dog, and when a man has only one dog, the pressure is doubled. A canny handler runs his weaker dog when he judges the sheep will be most difficult (usually in the afternoon) and tries his best dog against the sheep that promise the most points.

If a handler has two experienced dogs and another, younger one gaining experience in the Nursery trials or farmed out to a hill shepherd for good hard daily work, that handler is a rich man. In the late 1970s, when John Angus ran his Cap and Ben, he was hard to beat. John Angus still dreams about those dogs.

Flint's right eye, John Angus said, had gone opaque and sore. "The poor bugger keeps pawing at it and making it worse."

The greatest difficulty handlers of John Angus's ability have is finding a proper dog to work with. Such dogs are scarce and quite expensive—a dog like Taff would take five months of a hill shepherd's wages. In the balmy past, hill shepherds had to sell their best dogs to wealthier farmers and trial men. They simply couldn't afford to keep them.

John Angus's farm, Kiltyrie, lies two miles past Killin in the central Highlands. Like many pretty Scottish villages, Killin depends on the tourist trade, and this early on a weekday morning, tourists scramble over the rocks, photographing the falls of the Dochart.

Kiltyrie Farm sits on the slopes of Ben Lawers, the second highest mountain in Great Britain, a venerable overfold with its head in the mist. Since 1975, it's been part of the National Trust, and a public road proceeds through John Angus's land to the Visitor's Center. "All day they go up the hill and then they come down," John Angus grumbles. "Up and down."

The National Trust won't allow John Angus to use his tractor where it might scar the vegetation. The public road is unfenced, so the sheep have free passage to the high ground, and occasionally a car kills a lamb and (since ewes huddle on the dark warm road at dusk) tourists sometimes run over a ewe. "There's bloody nothing up here for the buggers to see," John Angus says.

Generally, hill farms have one or two flat fields where they can sow swedes (rutabagas) or silage oats, but Kiltyrie is either uphill or downhill; the only level is the narrow terrace for the house and byre.

Five years ago, John Angus MacLeod and Helen Smeaton bought the place with insurance money after their hotel, the Altnacealgach, burned down. Kiltyrie's previous owners had been carried out feet first, and the farm was in terrible shape. The sheep flock was a disaster.

Most hill farms contain three or four thousand acres of unfenced upland ground. Because grazing is poor, the ewes spread out on the slopes and hilltops. The ewes are inspected frequently (during lambing, twice daily) by the shepherd; when anything is found wrong with them, it must be put right on the spot, whatever the visibility or weather. If a ewe is having lambing difficulties, the shepherd must catch the ewe and deliver her. If a ram has got in with the wrong hirsel, he must be returned to the proper one. When a ewe goes down with ketosis or mastitis, she must be treated from the modest pouch the shepherd slings over his shoulder. The Scottish hills are veined with burns and drains (ditches). Not infrequently, a ewe will tumble into a drain onto her back and be unable to regain her feet. The ewe is said to be "cowped." Her rumen compresses her lungs, and unless she is helped to her feet, she will suffocate. Some sheepdogs are particularly good at locating cowped ewes. A few will actually tug them back onto their feet.

John Angus and Helen run 2,300 ewes on Kiltyrie, a high stocking rate for ground whose vegetation is principally heather, peat moss, and gorse. They've put all their money into improving their flock. They haven't done much with the farmhouse, nothing at all with the narrow stone byre.

Kiltyrie farmhouse is a commodious white stone building with a patched slate roof. Several windows have been replaced with painted plywood sheets with faux window frames drawn on.

The farmhouse is perched above Loch Tay, and Helen jokes that they should put a warning sign on the roadside. "The tourists come over the wee rise and see all *that* and they brake to take a photo and are smashed from behind, oh there's been three or four smash-ups there. . . ."

Helen Smeaton and John Angus have lived together for eight years, since Helen came to manage his Altnacealgach Hotel. John Angus didn't mind guiding the hotel's fishermen, but lacked interest in the day-to-day management. He didn't care for tourists and enjoyed being an innkeeper only in the off-season, wintertime, when the locals would come in for a wee dram of an evening.

Helen's a dark-haired, dark-eyed woman who likes good crack or a laugh. Last Saturday, at a rather stuffy wedding reception, Helen was dancing with Pat McGettigan. Pat's old friend, a sheepdog man himself. Though you wouldn't guess it from his dancing, Pat has a wooden leg. Pat stepped on Helen's foot. Helen gave the wooden leg a frightful kick and cried, "If you can't put that bloody thing on straight, I'll straighten it out for you," and knelt, there on the dance floor and jerked and twisted at Pat's leg, the two roaring with laughter while the proper (and very English) guests gaped at the pair of them.

Helen keeps Kiltyrie's books, orders the supplies ("Some salesman will stop, and John will say, 'Oh

Helen, this fellow wants to sell us our winter nuts (feed),' and I'll have to say, 'John, I ordered our nuts in July' "). Helen has tea and cheese sandwiches and biscuits for us when we arrive.

Grampian is the Scottish National Television Service, and its sheepdog-trial trophy stands on John Angus and Helen's livingroom sideboard, flanked by bottles of eight-year-old malt whiskey, "bottled especially for Grampian Television." There are other sheepdog-trialing trophies here and there, and three sets of deer antlers over the mantle. John Angus has been a shepherd stalker in his time, guiding sportsmen after deer when he wasn't tending the sheep. In the back part of the house, the parlor contains more of John's trophies, large and small, unpolished. Most sit where they were set down when they came into the house.

Helen is a strongly built woman in her thirties. She's big boned, not fat, and she goes straight to the point. Kenny Gibson, the dog trainer, nicknamed her the Buffalo.

As usual, there are house guests at Kiltyrie—a couple of Welshmen, Helen tells me. They're out this afternoon, touring the countryside.

John Angus says, "The sheep at Blair Atholl tomorrow are going to be bloody desperate. They have them from a man who works them from a motorbike, and his only dog is a hunter" (a hunter is a crude working dog who barks the sheep up the hills). "Christ, they'll be hellish at the pen."

"You can wave your bonnet at them, John," Helen says and John Angus laughs.

At the Wharton trial, it seems, the sheep were very light (skittish) at the mouth of the pen, quite unwilling to enter, and Flint was too strong a dog for the situation. If John Angus asked Flint to force them, they'd bolt. If he did nothing, they'd stand in the mouth of the pen until the timekeeper called "Time, John." So John

Angus removed his fore-and-aft and dangled it from the tip of his shepherd's crook and delicately, oh, so delicately, waggled it in the lead ewe's face. Faced with pure lunacy, this weird *thing* on a stick, the ewe backed into the pen and her mates followed.

Helen shook her finger, "After she'd sniffed the bonnet, John. It was the sniff made her retreat."

While John Angus phoned the veterinarian about Flint's eye, I chatted with Helen. I admired her new kitchen cabinets, and she said they were secondhand, weren't they handsome? A Welsh carpenter had come to stay with them on holiday, and while his family had toured about, he'd installed them.

Recently, they'd had Helen's mother for a fortnight's visit. When younger, her mother had fussed over every poor or sickly soul in the village and now, older and infirm herself, she'd become depressed.

I said something banal about the difficulty of growing old.

Helen said, "People hate to grow old when they didn't do what they wanted when they were young."

John hopped Flint into the boot, and we set off for the veterinarian in Aberfeldy. I asked John Angus how Taff's pups were doing.

A strong pup sired by a dog like Taff can fetch seventy-five pounds, and stud fees aren't an insignificant part of a sheepdog man's income. Some first-rate trial dogs are indifferent to bitches, a few are sterile, and many don't breed true. The only way anyone can predict how a pup may turn out is to inquire about previous litters. My question, thus, had to do with John Angus's financial prospects and reputation.

All intelligent queries about top sheepdogs are highly charged and frequently answered with imperfect candor. John Angus said, "Taff's pups have a bit of a grip in them until they're ten or eleven months old. But then you say, 'Stop that, Doggy,' and they stop."

John Angus paid two thousand pounds for Flint. Tony Illey, who owned Flint, sold him because he wouldn't go well away from home. Flint was a powerful worker on home ground with familiar sheep, but on the strange ground of a sheepdog course, under pressure, Flint got confused. John Angus (and his bank manager) took a big chance with Flint.

No two sheepdog trial courses are alike. The trial at Peebles is held in the municipal park; at the Royal Agricultural Show in Edinburgh, the trial is held in an arena. Some trials are held on hills so steep the dogs have to clamber to reach their sheep.

Since it was first held in 1906, the International Sheepdog Trial has rotated among England, Scotland, and Wales. The International is not the most venerable sheepdog trial, but is, undeniably, the most important. The site is changed each year, and that's how the trial comes to be named as the "Chester International" or the "Woburn Park International." This is the second time the International is to be held at Blair Atholl Estate. It was previously here in 1982. Sheepdog men and their families take this occasion for a family holiday, and all the B & Bs in Blair Atholl Village and nearby Pitlochry have been booked since July.

In August, National trials were held in Scotland, Ireland, England, and Wales. Hundreds of dogs compete for slots on the National team, and John Angus just squeaked in. The sheep were hopeless that afternoon, and he finished with eight seconds to spare. Helen admits to smoking three cigarettes during his fifteen-minute run.

The dogs that run at the International Sheepdog Trial are the most brilliant dogs in the world.

The veterinarian gives John Angus an antibiotic cream for Flint's eye and if it isn't improved in two days, he's to bring Flint back in. John Angus tells the vet about the flat trial course at Blair Atholl and about the sheep, previously owned by a man who shepherded from a motorbike.

When we return to Kiltyrie, John lets all the dogs out for a run. Besides Flint and Taff and Helen's dog, Dougie, he keeps a bitch and three half-grown pups in the straggly metal-roof byre. The dogs are kenneled in old milking stalls. Two slaughter hogs have quarters in the byre, too.

John Angus perches on an overstuffed chair in the sitting room and unwinds the bandage round his left leg. The leg is purple and shiny, and the ulcer on his calf is the size of a half dollar. John Angus is impatient with his wound (ulcerated varicose veins) and impatient with Helen when she tries to help. "Christ, what a thing! Will you look at it!" He hurls the soiled bandage in the fire. The leg isn't too painful when he wears low shoes, but his high green wellies rub against it. Helen rolls a clean sock over the fresh bandage and John tugs on his wellies and jumps Taff into the boot, "All right Dougie," and Dougie jumps in, too.

Since spring, Taff and Flint have been touring Scotland and the Borders in the Renault's boot. It is their dark cave, their refuge. In Britain, it is illegal to transport dogs this way, but most sheepdog men do it anyway.

Kiltyrie is forty-five minutes from Blair Atholl. We pass ruins of fortified houses and the grassy mounds of ancient hill forts. At Fortingall, we turn north. Fortingall boasts a first-rate ornamental blacksmith. "You can't get him to do ironmongery on the farm," John Angus says, rather pleased by the smith's stubborn self-definition. Pontius Pilate was born in Fortingall, legend has it, of a Roman officer and a Celtic girl.

Most of the hills are high and bare, but some are furrowed from summit to base; rows of furze where the Forestry Commission has planted trees. In some Scottish districts, 30 percent of the hills have been planted in spruce plantations. Endless rows of trees, neat as carrot tops, muffle the hills' stark outlines and change a way of life dominant in the Highlands since the Clearances.

In 1745, after Bonnie Prince Charlie and his highlanders were defeated in Culloden by the Duke of Cumberland (known thereafter as "the butcher"), his soldiers pulled down crofters' cottages, raped their women, and slaughtered their sons. It was a hard and bitter time. But nothing changed the Highlands so dramatically as did the importation of one of God's gentler creatures. It wasn't armed men who changed the Highlands. It was sheep.

Hardy Cheviots and Scottish Blackfaces bared the hills of shrubs and sapling trees. The overgrazed woods died, and the hills revealed their stoney naked outlines.

For two hundred years, sheep have occupied the dominant ecological niche here. Foxes and hoodie crows survived to prey on young lambs. Roe and fallow deer roam.

Forty years after Culloden, in the great glens where communities had lived, a few scattered shepherds grazed their flocks among the crofters' shattered byres, the fire-blackened lintel stones.

In some respects, those who have the daily use of a thing own it, and these shepherds, desperately poor though they were, were kings of this high barren land.

More than one present-day Scottish shepherd has told me of an affinity shepherds feel for the American cowboy, his resourcefulness and solitude.

But the cowboy's reputation for violence (however deserved) has never been part of the shepherd's mystique. Johnny Bathgate manages Easter Dawyck near Peebles in the Borders. He frequently comes to the States to judge sheepdog trials and once, in California, attended a spring roundup. "Oh they chased the calves down on horses and roped them and threw them down and wrapped these ties. . . ." He made a wrapping motion.

"Pigging strings?"

"Oh, aye. Around the feet and then another cowboy stepped forward with a red-hot iron and marked the beast." Johnny paused for a second, his gentle eyes wide. "We couldn't do that over here," he said. "They wouldn't permit it."

Last spring when I first came to Kiltyrie, John Angus and Kenny Gibson were in the byre sorting potatoes. Helen Smeaton was away on holiday, and the household looked it. Her dog, Dougie, made his bed in a mound of unwashed clothes beside the washing machine.

After weeks on the road, honest work was a relief and I squatted to help with the potatoes. John Angus said he was away to the Luss trial in the morning and would return to Kiltyrie to collect Kenny and then to the Assynt trial that afternoon, did I want to come? Of course I did.

That evening, I followed when John Angus took Flint and Taff up Ben Lawers. Every day the sheep would drift down the hill, and at 7 P.M., Taff would drive them back above the tourist road.

There aren't many men running in sheepdog trials in Scotland, three hundred perhaps. The dangerous handlers compete frequently, every weekend, and when the season heats up in June, there are midweek trials as well. To be eligible to run in the Scottish National, a dog must have won one open trial or captured several seconds and thirds.

Purses are small, twenty-five or thirty pounds for a first, and during a season, a handler is lucky if purses pay his gas money. Many farmers won't hire a shepherd who trials, fearing the trial man will worry his sheep training young dogs. Also, farming doesn't respect weekends, and the trialist has his weekends booked two months in advance.

We were off for Luss before sunrise, tea and buttered rolls in our bellies. Lorries, coaches, and caravans slowed our progress along the scenic lochs, and it was eight o'clock before the road widened along Loch Lomond.

I talk about the differences between Scottish sheep and American ones. I talk about American dog handlers and describe dog trials I've watched in Australia.

John Angus doesn't hear a word. "Bloody Hell," he says. "There'll be water in that wee burn today. At Luss, man. The sheep will balk on the crossdrive."

Although Loch Lomond is below the trial field, we can't see the loch from the course. When we arrive, the course is laid out, with gates and pen, but nobody else is here yet. John Angus lets Flint and Taff out of the boot. "Come along, Donald."

In recent years, televised sheepdog trials have become popular here. The Grampian trials are small beer, but the BBC's "One Man and His Dog" has been a phenomenon. Hosted by Phil Drabble, a countryman with an uncanny resemblance to a Toby mug, and Eric Halsell, whose prim commentary deplores each mistake ("Points off! There'll be points off for that!"), "One Man and His Dog" is an invitational trial run on scenic courses, generally, as John Angus notes, "with some bloody castle in the background." The Luss course has been laid out, it seems, with the scenic televised trials as a model. The dogs must slip through a gap in the hedge to find their sheep and fetch the sheep back through a fetch gate athwart a culvert. The dogs must push the sheep up a steep bank, and during the crossdrive, the sheep must leap a skinny water-filled burn. John Angus drops a tuft of wool where he wants his sheep to cross the burn.

We go through the hedge gap, up the course with Flint and Taff. There's a grove of trees between us and the waiting ewes. "They are fanatical about trees here," John Angus says. "They won't cut a limb off a tree so a dog can see his sheep. He walks Flint and Taff above the trees showing them where they'll need to go for a perfect run. We return straightaway to the car, and he pops them in the boot.

In the States, it's forbidden to take your dogs on a trial course before they run, but I say nothing because I'm sure it's the same here.

We take a drink of coffee from John Angus's thermos as other handlers start to arrive. Several walk the course. I notice one man drop his own tuft of wool. Soon enough there are fifteen or twenty cars drawn up at the foot of the course; handlers stand about warming their hands in their pockets and talk dogs and sheep, sheep, sheep. Running according to prearranged order, they'll trickle in all day long. Few will stay for the entire trial. Most, like John Angus, will run at other trials later in the day; Peebles, perhaps, or Carsphairn.

To test the course, John Angus will run Flint first. As Flint goes through the hedge, John Angus plans to give him a "wee safety whistle" to push him out until he's beyond the trees.

When John Angus steps to the handler's post, all the worries drain right out of him and he is at ease. He takes all the time he needs to set Flint up properly, and then Flint's off! Flint goes through the hedge and takes the "wee safety whistle," but when he comes upon the pen where sheep wait before they're released onto the course, he thinks these are the sheep John Angus has sent him for and he freezes right there. Peremptorily, John Angus whistles Flint by, onto the proper five sheep, blackface ewes, who bounce down the course but jam at the fetch gate, unwilling to clamber up the steep bank.

At my elbow, a handler murmurs, "That dog's dear at two thousand pounds."

Another replies, "That dog's dear at a thousand pounds."

But Flint masters his sheep, brings them in, and begins his drive. Twice, the sheep come off proper line, but Flint gets them through the obstacles. John Angus and Flint get a quick shed and clap the ewes in the pen. As John Angus comes off the field, he's fuming at the course's designer and the trial committee, and several Scots gather round, all wearing that strange sly smile.

"Oh bloody hell. A hellish course! What fool set up a course so the dog must pass the release pen to find his sheep? Oh, you'll never see me at this bloody trial again."

A few minutes before he's to run Taff, John Angus takes him out in the woods to relieve himself, to stretch his legs. When they go to the post, John Angus changes his mind and sets the dog off on the left side where we didn't go this morning. Taff runs out well to a drystane wall, follows the wall until he strikes a wire fence, jumps the fence, and starts to come in perfectly on his sheep but then stops short and begins to drive the sheep away, just as he does every evening with Kiltyrie's ewes on Ben Lawers. "Taff! Taff. Come by, Taff." And Taff arcs around behind them and thereafter runs an impeccable course.

When John Angus comes off, he puts Taff in the boot. "Well boys, we're off to Assynt." In the car, John Angus notes, "If Taff'd had a proper outrun, he would have been hard to beat. Bloody course!" He slapped his horn at a sluggish lorry.

We're back at Kiltyrie by noon and snatch a roll and cheese and a cup of tea. Kenny Gibson isn't feeling well and can't come, so John Angus grabs the Assynt trophy (he won the trial last year), drops it in a paper bag, and we're off.

The roads John Angus chooses are invariably the most direct, the crookedest, and slowest. We swoop across the hills on bare-bones single tracks; the Renault grunting up one steep rise after another. John Angus frets about Flint. Kenny Gibson has offered to take Flint for six months to settle him, but, of course, John Angus needs two dogs. John Angus recalls Glen, the dog who came fourth at the Scottish National when he was eleven years old. At the shedding, John Angus was running out of time. From the grandstand, Raymond MacPherson called out, "Be Quick!" (in Gaelic) and John Angus cried Glen in and Glen jumped over the backs of the sheep to shed off the correct one.

Gloomily, John notes, "Flint'd nae manage that."

We seem to be traversing the spine of the earth. It is spare up here, and since John Angus travels with my window open, cold. The sun casts short shadows as we race along. John Angus is instantly less confident once we turn onto the A9 motorway near Tummel Bridge. There are too many cars, all traveling too fast. John worries about Flint stopping for the wrong lot of sheep at Luss. He frets about Taff.

Until he bred Don, Perry MacKenzie wasn't a trial man. One fine spring day, Perry and Don came upon a neighbor in trouble. Hector, a crusty old herd, grazed his flock along Loch Inver, a sea loch. One ewe had taken her lamb out to a rock and the tide came in and there they were, the two high and dry. Perry asked Hector if he should send Don after them, and Hector said, "No dog can kep yin beast off that rock, but ye're welcome to try."

Perry gathered a few other ewes at the water's edge to serve as a magnet before he sent Don. Don swam out into the loch and came behind the rock. Glaring at the ewe, he got one paw up, then another, until he had full purchase, and—an inch another—he backed her until she tumbled off the rock and swam for shore with her lamb after.

Hector was lavish with praise, "I've never seen a dog to do that before. Yin's a grand dog. A grand beast."

Perry wasn't above priming the pump. "You think so, then?"

"Oh, aye, I do. A grand dog, Don. I've never seen better."

"I've been thinking of entering him in the sheepdog trials."

"Oh aye, aye."

"Do you think he'd do well at the trials?"

Hector shot Perry a look and said, exactly, "Aye. Any fool could win with a dog like that."

John Angus smacked his leg and repeated the punch line, "You see, Donald, any *fool* could win with a dog like that."

About two in the afternoon, we arrived at Loch Assynt in the northwest Highlands. This was John Angus's old stamping grounds—his hotel hadn't been far from here. The course was laid out on the loch shore; a great hill loomed on the far side. An aluminum caravan served as the trial secretary's headquarters, and behind the caravan a table displayed all the trophies, plus bottles of whisky and bags of dogfood to be raffled off. The hill shepherds had come away from their flocks, local citizens were enjoying the spring sunshine, and children dodged among the parked cars. Everybody knew John Angus, and he joked and cracked and didn't walk the course or fret about the sheep.

I was wearing my Texas hat, which is appropriate attire for sheepdog trials in the States, and the Scots asked me about them. Yes, we have a good many trials. We have some good dogs, yes. Sometimes you Scots make a mistake and export a good one. Laughter.

The beer tent was busy, and some had spent more time in its shelter than their livers required. One neat young man in impeccable plus fours introduced himself and admired my hat, "We need a dash of color," he said. "No offense." When I said I'd come with John Angus, the young man said he personally owed John Angus a great debt and I could tell John Angus so. Would I have a wee dram?

Hamish MacLean ran his bitch, Lynn, who came fourth at last year's International. I got a couple hamburgers from the luncheon caravan (they don't taste the same over here). Beside the cashbox, they have post-cards for sale: a single sheep exiting the shearing shed, flying in her glee, literally flying: all four feet in the air.

John Angus takes Flint out several times to talk to him and show him the sheep. When Flint runs, he's erratic at first, but settles toward the end.

At one time, Hamish MacLean was a good-enough piper to play for the Alec Guinness film, *Tunes of Glory*. Alec Guinness is a fine man, Hamish says. Once the filming was done, the actor took all the pipers to dinner. Hamish no longer plays the pipes, "The dogs do nae care for them."

At the Edinburgh trial, last summer, while Hamish MacLean was trying to get his sheep shed, a dachshund whipped onto the course, yapping. Without pause, Hamish bent, scooped up the little dog, tucked it under his arm like the bag of his bagpipe, and squeezed the little snout shut while concluding his work.

Perry MacKenzie and Hamish are great pals. At the crossdrive, Perry MacKenzie retires Don and comes off the course, "I retire when the dog's no longer pleasing me," he said.

"Is that so? Would you retire, then, if the dog was not pleasing you but you had lost no points? Would you retire then?"

Perry says he would surely retire, he would surely.

John Angus's Taff has a wonderful run until the pen, when one ewe refuses to go into the pen with the others. Taff finally presses her in but has lost most of his pen points by the delay.

When John Angus comes off the course, he says, "The moment I saw that blue kidney, I knew we were for it. Damn the brute."

Hirsels are identified by distinctive crayon marks. Four of John Angus's sheep had shoulder marks; the stroppy ewe was marked blue on the kidney. Since her running mates were strangers, the blue-kidney ewe wished to have nothing to do with them, and her stubbornness at the pen ruined Taff's run.

With the loch, the blue hills, and the sunlight, the citizens sniffed the air and told one another how lovely it was. They were full of innocent self-congratulations.

The young man in plus fours came to tell me, once again, how much he owed John Angus. "He doesn't speak about it, but it's true."

Later, when I asked John Angus, he sighed, "That lad will stay drunk all day," he said. "He comes from a good family, too."

After the last run, notables give out trophies and envelopes with prize money, and as each place is announced, there's a flurry of applause. Taff is third, Flint is seventh. There's a chill in the air. Three men fold the beer tent and bag the empty cups and pint cans. Prizes are awarded to the youngest handler and to the oldest. "And for the *loudest* handler!" To hoots and applause, a young man is awarded a two-foot sausage. The whisky and dogfood are raffled off, the Trial Committee and Secretary applauded.

The Assynt Hotel is situated on a rise above the loch and they're sorry, but so early in the season, they only serve dinner for guests.

The young man in plus fours comes out of the hotel bar and passes us without speaking. He wobbles his bicycle down the lane until he falls. He dusts himself off and walks the bicycle around the turn.

Villages are far between up here, and we don't stop until Ullapool, where we're almost too late for service. It's a midsize seafood restaurant, full of young people and their dates on a Saturday night. While I look over the menu, John Angus takes our small change to the pay phone, ringing handlers who ran at Luss. When he returns, he says that after we left Luss, the sheep got very difficult, so Taff, despite his flawed outrun, is in the prize list.

After Ullapool, I take the wheel, scaring the daylights out of John Angus. (I still have trouble judging the left verge with right-hand-drive cars.) I do better on the A9, opening the car up to the limit and cruising right along. The car is an isolated world, lit by the gauges, the infrequent headlights of overtaking cars. John Angus talks about the hotel he had, how damnably difficult it was. There were legal problems and questions about the fishing rights, and it was difficult collecting the insurance after the fire. I talk about my life, my farm.

At Tummel Bridge, we come off the motorway, and John wants to drive. The roads are no wider than before, no less steep. Sheep are bedded down in unexpected dips. Our tires crunch across mats of their droppings.

On top of the highest ridge, John stops and we get out for a pee. From here, I can't see a light on any horizon. John Angus lets Taff and Flint out so they can have a pee, too. The sky is very big, bounded by the silhouetted hills. Taff's ears perk up when he hears a distant sheep bleat.

Kenny Gibson has fed and exercised the dogs so there's nought to do after we pull in to Kiltyrie. Since daybreak, we've traveled nearly five hundred miles and it's 2 A.M. Taff's third at Assynt paid twenty-two pounds, Flint's seventh, seven. As I went up to bed, John Angus said, "You can sleep in tomorrow, Donald. The Falkirk trial won't start until nine."

When I returned to Scotland, eight months later, speeding over some of the same roads toward the Blair Atholl International, I recalled the spring day John Angus trialed Luss and Assynt in one day. John Angus said, "Aye. Assynt is a lovely trial."

I said, "The roads look better in the daylight."

When nineteenth-century scientists began ranking animals by intellect, they were perplexed by the dog.

Chimpanzees and other primates were physically most like humans, exhibiting "human behaviors": problem solving, tool making, and the like. But, unlike the dog, chimps were useless. (And nineteenth-century men had a broader experience of useful animals than we do today.) In *Mental Evolution in Animals* (1883) zoologist George Romanes ranked dogs and apes equally, below only humankind.

Other theorists made capital of a blurry meaning. "Ah yes," they said. "The ape is more *intelligent,* but the dog is more *sagacious.*" This stroke pleased abstract thinkers and practical livestock men alike. The root of sagacity is "a keen attention to the sense, particularly the sense of smell," but, of course, the word has come to mean rather more than that.

The Border Collie has been called "the wisest dog in the world." The shepherd's dog, described in Dr. Caius's *British Dogges* (1570) sounds very like the Border Collie of today:

This dogge, either at the hearing of his master's voyce, or at the wagging and whistleling in his fist, or at his shrill and hoarse hissing, bringeth the wandring weathers and straying sheep into the selfsame place where his master's will and wish is to have them, whereby the shepherd reapeth the benefit, namely, that with little labour and no toyle or moving of his feet he may rule and guide his flocke according to his owne desire, either to have them go forward, or to stand still, or to drawe backward, or to turn this way or to take that way. . . .

No doubt, breeding the shepherd's dog in the sixteenth century was a rough business. When early shepherds needed a turn of speed, they probably looked to the whippet or greyhound, and the Border Collie's implacable glare, its "eye," is descended from the hunting dog's point. (Sometimes, approaching his sheep, a Border Collie will freeze, one foot in the air. When a pointer does this, he's praised. In a Border Collie, it is called "sticky.")

When collies came from the Borders to the Highlands during the Clearances, their skills were stretched by necessity. Valued dogs had keen hearing (at a mile, it's hard to distinguish command whistles from bird calls), great stamina (a dog on a gather can easily traverse a hundred miles of rough ground in a day), and a desire to herd.

Until this century, there was a fair variety of working stock dog breeds. Drovers' dogs brought the livestock to market; there, market dogs chivvied them from pen to pen, and many British counties had their own distinct collies.

Like the Welsh Grey and the Dalesman, most of these collie types are probably now extinct. Others, like the Shetland and rough collie, have been taken up by show breeders and are virtually useless for livestock work.

The Border Collie has been saved as a work dog by being beneath human vanities. Nobody could look at this utilitarian, peasant's dog and say, "What a noble head!" or "Also owned by several crowned heads of Europe." Until recently, in Britain the dog wasn't showed at all. Its breeding was left in the hands of agriculturists, who founded the International Sheepdog Society to "promote and foster the breeding, training and improvement in the interests and for the welfare or benefit of the community of the breeds or strains of sheepdogs, to secure the better management of stock by improving the shepherd's dog. . . ."

Breeders who select the stud dogs and bitches within a breed effectively direct the breed's progress, and among sheepdogs, the eminent dogs have been those who excelled at sheepdog trials. The ISDS has always been directed by practical stockmen (J. M. Wilson was made an M.B.E., not for his expertise with sheepdogs, but for improvements he made in the Scottish Blackface), and these men were (and are) largely indifferent to a dog's appearance if the dog could get the job done. The ISDS has no conformation standard for sheepdogs and (theoretically) if your Rottweiler was trained to such a standard that it could win a major sheepdog trial, it could be registered with the ISDS. Several Bearded Collies have been so registered in the past.

There is a strongly held belief that a Border Collie often resembles its dominant ancestor. You hear of a "Gilchrist spot type" or "Bosworth coon markings." The first time Davey McTeir took his Ben to a trial, an old herd came over. "I've a bitch to put to your dog," he said.

Astonished, Davey asked, "Don't you think you'd like to see how he goes before you decide?"

"Oh, no need. No need. Your dog's the very image of Wilson's Cap. It's taken thirty years to make another one."

It's worth noting that McTeir's Ben went on to win the Scottish National in 1972 and did become an eminent sire.

It is possible to think of circumstances where other breeds of stock dog can outperform the Border Collie. In close work (pens, yards, and chutes) in Australian summer heat, the kelpie (another variety of collie) has more stamina than a Border Collie. When you wish to drive a great number of sheep up narrow trails, a hunter is more useful than a Border Collie. A hunter's barking hastens the whole flock along, while a Border Collie's silent intimidation can pressure only the last ewe in line. In New Zealand, the Huntaway is a distinct breed. In Scotland, most hunters are Border Collies who've been trained to bark on command.

These exceptions noted, the Border Collie is the most frequently employed livestock dog in the world. Trials are held in South Africa, Australia, the United States, Canada, France, the Falklands, and Switzerland. Johnny Bathgate exports most of his dog's progeny to Scandinavia.

The Border Collie's singular ability is to work well (sagaciously?) at a great distance from his shepherd. This is a complex skill. Since the dog is often out of the shepherd's sight, he must work well on his own. Geoff Billingham said, "Even when my old Jed bitch was getting past it, I could still send her out to gather the Hill while I went inside to have my breakfast. When I'd finish and come out, she'd have them all down, in the steading."

Yet the dog must be willing to take instructions, too. One scientist claimed that the Border Collie was able to comprehend 274 distinct commands. This is, I think, a fair bit of nonsense. There are brilliant Border Collies and dullards. And it isn't clear what constitutes a command. When John Angus unlatches the boot and the dogs jump in, has he given them a command? When he's parked on the trial grounds and the boot is open for air and the dogs don't jump out, is this a command? When John Angus holds Flint's sore eye open so I can squeeze ointment directly onto the eyeball, what commands keep Flint from struggling or snapping at me?

When a Border Collie changes hands, his original handler will routinely make a tape of the dog's whistle commands so the new owner can get them exactly right.

Typically, a tape will contain whistles for

go left (comeby)
go right (away to me)
lie down

stand
pause
walk onto your sheep
go slow

You're too near, get out
You're too far, come in
This one (shed this sheep and hold it)
Go back (stop, abandon the sheep you presently have, go back [to the right or left] and seek a new lot)

These commands can be modulated. By tone, a shepherd can tell his dog whether he wants him to stop and stay or stop, but get back up again. He can tell the dog to go left a little, go left a lot, go left wide, or go left NOW. If you shut your eyes when a dangerous handler has a classy dog on the course, you'll hear assurances, insistences, demands, soothings. You'll hear who the man is and what he hopes his dog to be.

On the second day of qualifying at Blair Atholl, I will time the commands as Johnny Templeton directs Roy on his crossdrive. I count seventeen distinct commands in fifteen seconds.

In the late sixties, when J. M. Wilson was running Bill II, near at hand, he used the dog's name for commands. "Bill" meant "Go Left." "Bill-uh!" meant "Go Left, NOW." "Will-yum" meant "Go Right," and when J. M. wanted Bill to walk skittish sheep into the pen, at a tense moment, he'd pop his fingers . . . just *pop*.

In animal training, control is inversely proportional to distance. How biddable would the circus tigers be, uncaged, five hundred yards from the trainer with the whip? And when the family pet dog strikes a fascinating scent, your ability to halt the dog will depend on how near you are.

Davey Sutherland is estate manager at Borrobol, a 22,000-acre spread in the northern Highlands. Davey's unregistered Border collies, Bert and Bob, are on identical commands; Bert's "Go Left" whistle is the same as Bob's. The Borrobol hills are low, thousand footers, strewn with boulders. One day last fall, Davey brought both dogs along while gathering ewes. Davey lay Bert down, told him "Stay," and proceeded with Bob after the sheep. When Bob brought in the first hirsel, he missed a few, so Davey whistled "Go Back" and Bob found more, but still hadn't them all, so Davey whistled "Go Back" again. The sheep came off a steep ridge, Davey whistled Bob left and right, brought him on, told him "Go Slow." At such distances, mind, he was commanding a dot that was herding glints.

When Davey had the ewes down, he started for home but didn't find Bert where he'd left him. That was unusual, but Davey figured Bert had gotten frustrated and gone back to the farmhouse. When Davey and Bob got the sheep put away, no Bert. Before Davey could get worried, a neighbor phoned. "Are you missing a dog?"

Anxious to do his part, Bert had taken Bob's first "Go Back" whistle and topped the hill as the second "Go Back" sounded. The first sheep he found were in a neighbor's paddock, and Bert began working the sheep to and fro to Davey Sutherland's whistled commands.

The neighboring farmer said it was lucky he knew Bert. He would have shot a strange dog. As it was, the neighbor thought Bert had gone mad, chivvying the sheep back and forth to whistles only Bert could hear, from a shepherd 2½ miles away.

Blair Atholl estate, the venue of the 1988 International Sheepdog Trial, is 148,000 acres. Much of the estate is hill land, but there's lush bottomland, too, and that's where the trial course is laid out. It is rumpled slightly. Not quite "flat as a pancake."

When John Angus and I drove in, the evening before the qualifying trial, the grandstands were set up, six canvas-roof portable units stretched across the foot of the course. At the televised sheepdog trials, they set up remote cameras along the course so viewers could see the dog gather its sheep and fetch them, but here, as at most sheepdog trials, the judges, spectators, and handler can see only the inbye work (the drive, pen, and shed). The outfield work (outrun, lift, and fetch) are incompletely visible.

The dog handlers wore thigh-high green wellies and waxed-cotton waterproof jackets. Some wore waterproof leggings as well. It had been a wet summer. Some men walked the course. Some pointed out difficulties with the shepherds' crook they all carried. John Angus said a few hellos. One handler stood at the handler's post, envisioning the next day. Another tried the action of the pen's gate. A rope is attached to the gate and once the handler goes from the shedding to the pen and takes the rope (or gate), he cannot turn loose until all his sheep are in the pen and the gate is closed.

Neither pen nor gates are painted. Bright paint may alarm the sheep.

From the handler's post, you face a great unfenced meadow with rumples in it. There are dips and a copse of trees behind which the sheep and dog would be out of sight. The course is shaped like a butternut squash: one bulb with another, greater bulb atop it. From top to bottom, the course is thirteen hundred yards, and the widest part of the bigger bulb is nine hundred yards across. The qualifying runs will be held tomorrow and next day on the smaller bulb. The field is bordered on the right by a stone wall and beyond that the Scotrail right of way (Edinburgh-Inverness).

This had been a floodplain before it was a meadow. On the left, cattle and sheep grazed on the foothills. John Angus cocked an eye at the sky, "It'll be a fair day tomorrow," he asserted. "They're having the Lairg [lamb] sale tomorrow, and they've never known it to rain for that sale."

Dougie at our heel, John and I ambled round the course, trying to view each tussock, every dip, like a hurrying sheep might see it. John bent and picked up a tuft of wool someone had dropped. He grinned.

A Landrover came bumping out to where John Angus and I stood and a serious pale face poked out the window. "John, you know you're not to take a dog on the course before it runs."

"Oh hello, Ray. Hello."

Ray Ollerenshaw, O.B.E., chairman of the International Sheepdog Society.

John Angus smiled like the cat who ate the canary, like the trailing edge of tailfeathers were still protruding from his mouth. "Oh, no Ray. This is young Dougie. You'll remember I'm running Taff." He bent to give Dougie a pat. "Just giving Dougie a stroll around, Ray."

The Landrover withdrew.

At the fetch gates, John Angus cursed. The workmen who set up the course had driven the length of the field, creating deep ruts that ran straight for the fetch gates but swerved, in the last few feet, around them.

John Angus feared the sheep, coming straight for the fetch gates, would get in that track until the last moment when they'd swerve past the gates, and such is the caliber of the competition, that that miss would likely cost a man his chance to qualify.

Raymond MacPherson was worried, too. You could ask your dog to push them out of the ruts, but, "If I know Blackies, they won't turn unless you put a dog at their shoulder, and then the first two sheep will go [through the gate] and the second three will stop and run back up the course." John Angus hoped it would rain. If it rained, the ruts would fill with water and the Blackies would shun them altogether.

That evening, we lolled before the fire at Kiltyrie, sampling Grampian Television's malt whisky. John Angus told his two Welsh houseguests about the International course ("flat as a pancake"), the sheep ("herded by a bloody fool on a motorbike"), the ruts at the fetch gate.

One Welshman, (Mr. Jones) was a placid, smiling man who didn't speak much other than to say, " Yes, please, if you're having one, another."

The other Welshman (Mr. Evans) had been to America to show Welsh cobs. He'd thrice had the champion at the Royal Welsh Show. He was a vivid talker.

John Angus said the trial course for the Grampian had been too bloody small. He said that Michael Puegniz had walked a bitch in heat all over the course before the dogs ran. "Bloody man." He also said, "Taff'll give you a tight turn [at the drive gate], but I haven't the confidence in him I had in Old Ben."

The two Welshmen had been driving along the loch, when they spotted a dead stag on a shale hillside above the road.

"He'll be poached," John Angus averred.

Though in touring clothes, Mr. Evans saw a chance for a trophy and climbed to the beast. "It was bloody steep, mind, and I was slipping back as much as I was progressing and when I got to him, I had only this wee penknife, and he stank, how he stank, and the flies, and me cutting at his head with this wee knife, and the flies, and me not knowing how I was going to get it home if I did have it off. What a trophy he would have made."

9

The Big Course

I'm sure shepherds held impromptu sheepdog competitions prior to the sheepdog trial at Bala, Wales, in 1873. But Bala was the first modern trial, its course the same as today's. In the early days, trials were controversial. A few agriculturally minded aristocrats encouraged them, while more conservative farmers worried that their hired shepherds would waste time schooling their trial dogs on the farmer's good ewes. And, there were doubts the trials did what they claimed to do: select the best sheepdogs and bitches. Complaints persisted. In February 1916, a correspondent for *The Breeder's Gazette* wrote,

---

To be perfectly candid, I am afraid the trials as yet have not accomplished much. Doubtless they have interested a great many people in the shepherd and his collie, but that we have better dogs today than could be seen 40 or 50 years ago is a matter on which I am slow to pronounce judgement. Some features of present day working are certainly more clever and artful . . . but great, self-directed "hill-runs" are, I fear, less conspicuous than in the days of our fathers. The trials are doing nothing towards the production and development of the "sagacious" type of collie.

You'll hear that complaint today. However, as others have noted, few things improve a dog's skills more than an old man's misty memory, and there are grander dogs toasted in the beer tent than are seen on any trial course. There is no doubt that the International favors a certain type of wide-ranging hill dog, and the intensive trialing that brings a dog to the big course winnows out a good many dogs that would make first-rate work dogs and prepotent sires.

There are many fine working sheepdogs who cannot (or will not) tolerate the pressure of the trialing. Some will do it . . . grudgingly. John Angus feared Flint might be such a dog.

The designers of the sheepdog trials created a model of the work the dog does at home. As in all sports, the model is more precise, elegant, and difficult than the mundane activity it represents. Many competitive sports are mock-ups of warfare. Like other farmers' contests (ox pulls, plowing competitions) the sheepdog trial is a mock-up of work. After a poor trial, critical shepherds complain that "the standard of work wasn't what it should be." The highest praise a Scot will give a collie is, "Aye, yin's a useful beast."

Although spectators at the 1988 International have come from the United States, Canada, Holland, New

Zealand, as well as Britain, there'll not be many who don't have sheep and dogs at home. They are knowledgeable fans. The time limit for the qualifying trial is fifteen minutes, and as handlers run short of time and the timekeeper prepares to ring his bell, dozens of electronic stopwatches go off in the grandstands: *peep, peep, peep-peep, peeppeeppeeppeep.*

The handler goes to the post slightly paranoid, with a strong sense of urgency. Sheepdog trialing is a sport where points are taken away, never earned, and before you send your dog out, you have as many points as you'll ever have. Just behind you are four judges: one each from Scotland, Ireland, England, and Wales. A perfect (cumulative) qualifying score will be 440 points. Top scores will be in the three eighties and nineties.

Often as you walk onto the course, your dog will dash twenty yards ahead, looking for his sheep. Perhaps you clap your leg or call softly and the dog returns to your side. This is a time to settle yourself, swallow that lump in your throat, and see what you can learn as five sheep are herded (by two men and two dogs) to the let-out post, some four hundred yards in front of you. At that distance, you can't ken much, but you can certainly see if a ewe is trying to bolt. Is the whole lot fractious? Is a sick or elderly ewe lingering behind?

You meet your dog's eyes, and if you're right, your souls exchange confidence. The clock starts when you send him.

You can lose twenty points per judge on the dog's outrun. The outrun is the most important portion of the trial course and is judged strictly. What you hope is that the dog will cast out from your foot, widening himself as he nears his sheep, so he can come upon them from behind without startling them. Some dogs are born with a natural outrun: others must be trained to it.

The dog's life experience determines its gather. It

must have strong faith and have learned to delay gratification.

As the dog runs out, any command, by voice or whistle, is points off, and a man never signals his dog unless there's trouble to be avoided. The dog is racing away from its shepherd toward sheep it may have seen or may have been cued toward by the shepherd's stance and body language. As the dog goes out, he can easily lose sight of his sheep and, in dips and low places, certainly will. The dog's instinct tells him to come in; faith alone keeps him sailing out. If he yields and comes in too soon, he'll cross the course in front of his sheep and lose almost all his outrun points: disaster.

The dog must trust his shepherd to warn him when he's gone too far, when he's gone wrong. He must trust his shepherd's silence and keep on, widening, ever widening.

When an inexperienced dog finally finds his sheep, he'll rush in quickly, hoping to get to them and, usually, they will bolt like deer. A young Blackie can outsprint a dog for a hundred yards. Sometimes a hundred yards and a hiding place are all a ewe needs to beat a dog.

The experienced dog knows that slogging on farther, far beyond his ewes, before he turns in is initially more work, but nothing less works.

When the dog is behind the sheep, he stops of his own accord or is whistled to a stop.

If the outrun is correct, the first moment the sheep notice the dog is the lift. The lift is a test of perception and a clash of wills. Permit me this analogy: Picture yourself one morning, walking down the sidewalk, thinking about dailiness—your work perhaps, your wife's birthday, the postcard you intend to mail—when a car pulls to the curb and a stranger gets out and blocks your path. He (she) is strongly built and exudes menace. Although he (she) carries a weapon, it's not brandished. The stranger is dressed almost entirely in black, but there are small reassuring touches. Perhaps he wears a badge "Special Constable" or "Security." The stranger takes a step toward you.

If you are terrified, you may run or fight or bluster. If you are completely unthreatened, you may say, "Excuse me, please," and step around him.

If you turn and walk away, that's a perfect lift: full points.

When the sheep come away, with the dog trotting behind (or to one side or the other), the next portion of the course is an exercise in biddability. After the outrun, the shepherd is allowed to command, and most twitter like birds. Judges deduct points each time the sheep stray off the straight and narrow, if ever they pause or hurry. If, when they reach the fetch gate, they are deceived by the ruts and slip around the gate, that'll be 40 points gone. As the sheep come near the shepherd (and the throng of people immediately behind him), there is a three-species encounter. The sheep are frightened of the man, though more frightened of the dog. The dog has been a great distance out from the man and is relieved to be coming near again. The sheep approach a new, possibly dangerous animal, with a known quantity dogging their heels. This is the handler's best chance to settle everything, reassure the sheep (and dog), and read the sheep. Now he can see if one sheep is older or younger than the others. Which is the flock leader? Are any sheep out of condition, winded? Are they spooky or reconciled to being herded? At the same time, the handler must be preparing himself for a new, and quite different, phase of work: the drive. To the left, 150 yards ahead, at about ten o'clock, the drive gates await, and once the sheep come round behind the handler, he'll want to aim straight for the gap between those gates.

Tight turns are important in trialing, and the nearer the sheep come to the shepherd's feet as they pass around, the better.

For the sheep, coming around the handler is a great relief. Steadily they've been herded toward a man (danger) and a crowd of spectators (danger) and now, as they come around, this danger is suddenly behind them and they race away, sometimes leaping like lambs in the joy of their freedom.

This is a place where the young dog can easily go wrong. Its instinct is to run to the head of the flock and bring them back to the shepherd. Running sheep tease that instinct. If the dog succumbs, ignores his handler's commands, and fetches the sheep back, he will lose perhaps 80 of the drive's 120 points.

"Steady Cap! Cap, take time!"

Obedient to every instruction, the dog must herd the sheep directly through the drive gates. Once through the drive gates, another tight turn is called for. If the sheep are allowed to lollygag once they're through the gates, points will be lost. The dog must whip around and turn them onto the crossdrive.

The crossdrive crosses the course through the crossdrive gates on the handler's right, about two o'clock. Through the crossdrive gates, another tight turn and now the dog fetches the sheep to the man who can finally move from the handler's post into the shedding ring.

This ring is a forty-yard circle marked by clumps of sawdust. (Sheep have been known to balk at an unbroken sawdust ring.)

Like politicians, when threatened, sheep rush toward the center, the stronger pushing the weaker to the left or right. The very old and sickly are left outside the solid wooly mass for predator selection. Too bad for the senior citizens, but as a survival strategy, it works well.

To shed (separate) the sheep, the handler gets on one side of them, the dog on the other. The dog may charge through, physically splitting the flock or, more elegantly, dog and man may face the sheep from opposite sides and threaten them until they split apart. This strategy is as close to pure mysticism as anything I've seen on the trial field. Man on one side, dog on the other, they increase pressure gradually until the desired sheep squirt off from the others. Stuart Davidson, captain of the Scottish team, is a master of this maneuver.

The dog must dominate the shed sheep until it is clear that he could take them anywhere. Failed attempts, opportunities not grasped, allowing sheep to drift out of the shedding ring: All these cost points.

For the dog, asked to rush into the sheep while his partner harries them, the shed is reminiscent of the attack run his ancestor wolves once made before they settled down to a meal. The shed has great potential for a grip. If the dog grips a sheep, he is immediately disqualified, his trial is over, and man and dog retire.

Grips probably cause more disputes than any other element in a trial. On the hill there are practical circumstances when a dog needs to grip a stroppy old ewe, and most dogs will have a "Grip!" command. A few dogs have a different command to bring a ewe to her knees and hold her (to lamb her or medicate her). Nevertheless, grips are rarely tolerated on a trial field and at an International, never.

Time ticking away, the shepherd hurries to the pen. He'll clench the gate rope with one hand, extend his crook with the other. From left to right: crook, man, gate rope, open gate—these form an illusory wall blocking the ewes' escape while the dog presses them toward the mouth of the pen. The man is not permitted to touch the sheep.

Permit me to resume my analogy. Suppose that menacing black-clad stranger had followed you for half a mile, walking on one side of the street and the other, never so far back you could slip away and never so near that you'd run. Now, suppose his car reappears, the back door opens, and the stranger says, "In!"

The sheep know perfectly well that the pen is a trap. Penning them takes patience and a bodily understanding of the geometry of power. The sheep are less afraid of the man than of the dog. They are more afraid of the pen than of *either* man or the dog but not *both*.

If man or dog presses too hard, the sheep will fight or flee. Remember John Angus's bonnet on the end of his crook? Waggled in a skittish ewe's face, it was just queer enough to shift her. If the man comes on too strong, the sheep'll run around the pen. If the dog presses too hard, they'll duck under the rope or jump the man's crook.

Any waffling by the sheep at the pen mouth is points off. Any ewe who breaks around the pen is points off.

When you slam the gate of the pen, you take one glance at your stopwatch and go back into the shedding ring for the single. Mechanically, the single is like the earlier shed only more difficult. You and your dog will need to take that single ewe off with the speed and precision of a surgeon's knife. The ewe must not know what you intend, and when she turns and realizes she's out there all by herself—PREY—she must be held transfixed by the dog's glowing eyes, until her terror becomes paralysis and she is purely unable to take a step.

The judge calls, "Shed" or "That'll do," and it's all over. You come off the course to talk your run, to take orders for pups, to beeline to the beer tent for a wee dram. . . .

If you've done well, your dog walks happily at your side. If you've botched it, there's no sense saying "Good dog" and giving him a pat, no use in the world. Sheepdogs are undeceivable.

At Kiltyrie Farm, the morning of his qualification run, John Angus took his dogs out for a run; wrapped his ulcerated leg afresh; and put ointment into Flint's eye, which seemed to be improving, and Helen brought him his brogans, which she'd dried last night by the fire. When he complained his favorite jersey (a cable knit with suede patches at elbow and shoulder) wasn't clean, Helen said, "If you'd take it off sometime, I could wash it."

John Angus snapped, "Woman, you've a tongue that could sweep streets."

John Angus wouldn't run until 11 A.M., and Helen would ride to Blair Atholl, later, with the Welshmen. "John, somebody has to do things, here." John was anxious to be off. During the night it had rained, and had those ruts by the fetch gate filled with water, would the sheep be flighty or calm? How would they go for the first dogs?

The mist over Loch Tay had a blue tinge to it, like gunsmoke. The summit ridge of Ben Lawer was somewhere above the clouds. Billows of mist hung in the road and slowed our progress. I asked John Angus how much of his run he planned before he went to the post. "When you think about a thing in your mind, you can have a plan to combat it," he said.

A few minutes later, he said you'd just want to get finished with this course, no fancy work, just get finished.

Later, he estimated it'd take 360 points to qualify for the finals on Saturday.

As we race into Tummel Bridge, John Angus says he'll send Taff off before the sheep are all the way to the let-out post. If Taff picks them up before they're in line for the fetch gate, they'll be unlikely to get in the ruts. I ask if that won't confuse the men putting out sheep, to see a dog come sailing out, long before they expect him?

"Is this the bloody turn?" John cries, "Damn!"

We'd shot across the motorway and down the ramp on the other side. John braked, then wrestled us around, and we were back on the motorway again.

We park today on the hill above the course, and there're shepherds (in wellies and waterproofs and with crooks) taking admissions. When a handler wins a place on his national team, he's mailed a rectangular gold badge. Among the crowd today, I'll see shepherds and farmers whose badges read: Wales 1985, England 1987, Scotland 1978. Between trials, the badges are kept in the trophy cases in their dining rooms, along with the brilliant polished trophies and the photos of the kids and grandkids.

The badges also serve for admission. John Angus' Scotland 1988 lies dust covered in its glassine envelope on the dash. "Hold that up for them, won't you, Donald?"

From the hill, the entire course lies misty at our feet—the grandstands, secretary's tent, restaurant tent, beer tent, crafts-and-gift tents, and caravans for Chum Pedigree Dog Food (The Pro's Choice), the Alliance Insurance Company, and the Bank of Scotland.

The loudspeaker welcomes us to the 1988 Blair Atholl International and reminds us there are a good many sheepdog items on sale in the secretary's tent, as well as tickets for the International dinner tomorrow night.

On Thursday and Friday, the qualifying trials alternate members from each team, in reverse order of rank from their Nationals. The last shall run first. Bobby Short, a Scottish shepherd, and his three-year-old Bill (out of W. Stewart's Bob and his own bitch Gael) go to the post. The Blackies are light but not desperate. They are gimmers: yearlings after their first shearing. Most have pure-black faces, some are spotty black, and a few bear skinny horns. They are quick to sense a dog's weakness. Later, when Rob Kincade's Nan comes on too hard at the lift, the sheep fly down the course like banshees, and Nan never does get them settled.

When your run has gone wrong, is a complete disaster, your sheep flying this way and that and your dog no longer listening, you can't quit. You're out there as a member of the Scottish team, and if you walk off, all your team points are forfeit.

Over the years, the Scottish team has won most frequently, but the Welsh and English teams are formidable, too. Several men here have won the International before. Tim Longton, J. R. Thomas (nine scions of his great Don dog are entered in these trials), Raymond MacPherson, and John Templeton. Meirion Jones won the International in 1959 with his Ben dog, and this year, Jones' Spot has dominated the Welsh competitions.

I sit beside Peter Hetherington and his wife, Molly. Peter is a small, articulate shepherd, carefully dressed, who exports fifty dogs every year to America. Although Peter comes across frequently to judge our trials, he finds Americans deeply puzzling. One year he flew over with the dog that had just won the Scottish Nursery finals. "A bonnie dog, that."

It was in Texas. One spring afternoon, in his host's barn lot, they were training dogs—just fooling around, really—when a neighbor drove in. This man—he was a wealthy quarterhorse breeder—had never seen anything like these dogs. A revelation came to him. He asked, "Which one of these sumbitches is the best?"

Peter pointed to the Nursery champion.

The Texan said, "How much for the sumbitch?"

Purely to discourage him, Peter said he could have the dog for five thousand dollars.

Okay. The Texan went for his money belt, counted out the price, and chained the dog to a standard in the back of his pickup.

The next time he came to the States, Peter asked about the dog, who'd been one of the best dogs exported from Scotland that year. When the quarterhorse man had folks over for a barbecue, he'd send one of his hands down to the barn to turn three sheep out.

The dog'd race out and fetch them to the patio to his guests' applause. "A *good* sumbitch." Peter shook his head at the waste.

Mist clotted the field, and it was difficult to see the sheep at the top end. As they came down the course, the sheep bore to the left, so the dog had to be far left to keep them straight. Then, at the gate, they fell into the ruts, and the dog had to race to the other side very quickly, to push them out of the ruts and properly through.

Each of our small acts reveals us. When Johnny Templeton walks onto the course, he is quiet, diffident as a cleric. Alasdair MacRae strides to the post, dangles his crook from it, flips his coattails, and sets his fingers to his mouth for the first whistle. Stuart Davidson, once a champion Gaelic football player, goes to the post like the cock of the walk.

John Angus strolled out there like he and Taff were sharing a pleasant joke, all alone in the world. Taff swirled around to John Angus's left leg, asking to be sent that way, but he and John Angus had a wee chat, and Taff swirled to the right hand, all aquiver. John Angus whispered to Taff, asking him some questions, and Taff sailed out like the Bullet Train; I never heard the command.

John set himself in case Taff should need a correction on his outrun, but Taff went out, out, like he could have gone another five miles, and came around behind the sheep properly, and John whistled him down. Taff came onto them, came onto them, came onto them and They're Away! Flying down the fetch line, Taff was out, far to the left, counteracting their leftward lean; but surely Taff was too far, a hundred yards off his sheep. The sheep stayed on line approaching that fetch gate, ready to slip into the ruts. I'd swear it was too late when John Angus called Taff around to the right, Taff was too far away, couldn't possibly get there on time, but as the lead ewe tried to sneak around the gate, Taff arrived. "No," Taff said.

Startled by his materialization, the ewe draws up short, swerves, and now all the sheep are bolting across the back face of the gates, right past the gap, to the far side but John Angus brings Taff around to block them—"Not here either"—and, abashed, the sheep trot through the gap where they should have gone in the first place. All this to and fro had excited the sheep, and they picked up speed as they approached John Angus at the handler's post. The leading horned ewe was flock leader, and she didn't like the look of John Angus. She began to swerve wide and perhaps, here, John Angus might have taken a backward step to give the sheep more room, but he did not; he asked Taff to put more pressure on them, to keep the turn tight, and they whipped around John Angus and flew away from man, dog, crowd. In the grandstand I lifted my camera as the sheep sped toward the drive gate. Perfect! John Angus, Taff, five sheep, the gap in the drive gate; the line was so straight you could have laid a ruler on it.

Except for that to and fro at the fetch gates, Taff hadn't dropped a point. He had a brilliant run going: impeccable.

The next phase is the turn after the sheep go through the drive panel; a tight turn is required to bring the sheep onto the crossdrive. John Angus put his fingers to his lips for a whistle.

Five sheep hit the drive gate gap at once, running full tilt, the horned ewe slightly in the lead. John Angus whistled Taff around NOW! and Taff raced left around the outside of the drive gate and disappeared, right under the ewes' noses, and from where I sat, all I could see were the back ends of sheep; Taff was under their snouts somewhere. The sheep slewed, and one ewe (that horned ewe, it was) shot straight up into the air like a Harrier jump jet. She fell and scrambled to her feet, and as the sheep straightened for the cross-drive, Taff came into sight behind them and the crowd and I held our breath. Would the judges call a grip? Had they seen something we hadn't?

Whatever Taff had done in the face of those sheep had a salutary effect because they were stepping along the crossdrive, docile as could be. Quietly, John Angus whistled Taff on.

A single judge stepped out onto the course, lifted the bell, and rang it briskly, "That'll do, John."

John Angus turned, not really surprised. Confusion and anger warred on his face, and he opened his mouth and snapped it shut. He directed Taff to take the sheep where another dog could remove them from the course. Then he started toward the judges, then he halted, called Taff, and gave Taff a distracted pat. The grandstands applauded because it was hard, hard luck.

John Angus MacLeod and Taff came off the course to the shepherds waiting for them. John said, "That bloody horned ewe. That bloody, bloody bitch!"

Raymond MacPherson said, "Taff was already too tight when he came around you at the post."

Peter Hetherington said, "I warned you about that at the National, John. Taff was coming in too tight at the National."

John Angus said, "I never told you, but at the National, at the pen, Taff just clipped in and. . . ." John Angus made a jerking motion like a dog gripping wool. "The judges didn't see it."

Peter Hetherington shook his head.

John Angus said, "Taff was too tight Tuesday at the Grampian trial. That damned Michael Puegniz walking his bitch over the course like that, keying them up."

Helen stayed mum and when John turned toward the beer tent, she followed. "They couldn't have seen a grip," John Angus said. "*I* couldn't see it."

Peter said, "Aye, but she cowped, John. If yon ewe hadn't cowped, they couldn't have called it."

John Angus marched through the loiterers inside the beer tent, bought his dram, and drained it. He said to me, "I feel like cutting my throat." I couldn't meet his eyes.

It rains off and on as the qualifying continues. At noon, they set up the course for the brace trial. In the brace, the shepherd sets off two dogs and works them simultaneously. After his shed, he puts one lot of sheep in an open-mouthed pen and leaves a dog on guard while he puts the remaining ewes in a different pen. Stuart Davidson has a brilliant run with Craig and Moss. Both dogs are out of his Ben (a son of John Angus's Ben).

After four pairs run the brace, the singles trial resumes. The handlers' commands are sharp as dogs' barks. R. T. Goligher's Vic has what can be described as a temporary nervous breakdown. Vic does fine until the drive gate, when he whips to the sheep's heads and fetches them instead of driving as he ought. He takes his shepherd's corrections and gets the sheep back on track but skulks at their heels like a guilty teenager, turning his face toward Goligher for instructions at every step. This "keeking" is a fault. At the shedding ring, Vic won't come in because he feels so guilty and has become afraid of the sheep, and Goligher can't come off because he will lose team points, but he's dying out there, asking his dog and his dog refusing.

A pet Border Collie is tied to the fence, transfixed by the action before him. When his owner feeds him a cookie, he takes it to please her, but it dribbles out of his slack mouth.

There are Border Collie buffs at all the big trials. They're the ones with the funny hats with the Border Collie badges, the jerseys with alternating rows of shepherd's crooks, Border Collies, and sheep, the sweatshirts with legends ("Happiness is Spot") on the front side and a dog's blurry photo on the back. They are perfectly nice people who know more about the history of herding dogs than any shepherd in Great Britain. Some buffs own seven or eight Border Collies that they take on annual holiday to farms where the dogs can see sheep.

Some get obedience titles on their dogs (the Border Collie wins most of the obedience championships at Crufts), and some use their dogs for search and rescue or tracking. (One woman I know has her Border Collie trained to fetch a fresh roll of toilet paper.)

Many are careful to breed their bitches to the best working sires. It's hard to guess what the shepherds make of them. One woman told me her pup, Royce, was by John Templeton's Roy. "Roy's Royce," she said. "Get it?"

Johnny Bathgate is manager of a mixed (arable and livestock) farm not far from the Billinghams. From deep instinct, he is a kindly man, and his farm laborers take their meals at the same table as Johnny and his wife.

In the sixties, Johnny drove David McTeir and Jock Richardson to the trials. Of the three friends, only Johnny has never won an International. One spring afternoon, I watched Johnny work Vic, his powerful male, in a steep pasture above his farm. With anxious ewes and new lambs, Vic never set a foot wrong. Vic is as heartily muscular as Johnny Bathgate is gentle. I told Johnny he was a very lucky man.

When we came off the hill, Johnny put Vic up in the byre, in a straw-filled concrete kennel. The Bathgates keep a feist dog in the house, a Lhaso apso–terrier (?) mix, a matted, dancing, prancing beast with the full run of the furniture. I asked John if he ever let Vic in the house.

"But Vic's a collie," John replied.

Scots can be quite unsentimental about their Border Collies. Most weeks in the *Scottish Farmer*, retiring shepherds disperse their tools:

2½-year-old bitch,
    out of Davidson's Moss   £400
5-year-old bitch, works cattle   £200
18-month-old dog, trial potential   £800

Sometimes an aging eminent dog will be let into the kitchen to doze its days away by the fire, but, more often, dogs never see the inside of a house. I'm not sure whether this is the Scot's fastidiousness or respect. Most of the dog quarters I saw were clean and well furnished with straw, and perhaps it's not awful for a tired working dog to have a quiet place where people can't pester him.

Still, where the Forestry Commission has planted its blocks of dull overbearing conifers, among the ruins of shepherds' cottages and steadings, you can find hand-cut gravestones for these dogs, on a rise, where they'll be touched by the first warm rays of the morning sun. NELL. CAP. LOOS, ALWAYS FAITHFUL.

Spectators on the far left side of the Blair Atholl course had a better view of Taff's grip than did the judges or John Angus himself, and several said that when the horned ewe came through the gate so quick, Taff was right in her face and it was the other sheep piling up behind her who'd cowped her. Taff hadn't laid a tooth on her.

When John Angus tried that explanation on Johnny Templeton, Johnny Templeton said, no, Taff had got a hind leg, but later, in the car toward Kiltyrie, Helen protested, "Taff couldn't have done that. He's never done that in his life." That afternoon, she and John Angus had found an Irishman with no place to sleep and promptly invited him to Kiltyrie. We four were the only customers for late dinner at a pub in Aberfeldy. The Welshmen, Mr. Jones and Mr. Evans, had met up with their wives and were out for an evening of dancing.

Once they'd shown the Irishman his bed, John Angus and Helen let the dogs out for exercise. John Angus was awfully discouraged. "We keep too many dogs. Poor beasts, they're mad for work and we haven't it for them." He bent to pluck a twig from Taff's tail. "I should quit this stupid bloody business," he said.

We went in the parlor, and John Angus unrolled his bandage and kneaded his injured leg. John Angus said if he sold off the dogs, he wouldn't get much for them. "If a dog isn't good enough for John Angus," he said bitterly, "it isn't good enough for me. That's what they all say."

Helen drank tea.

John Angus said, "I've been neglecting the farm. I could get more work done here if I wasn't off dog trialing."

Helen said, "If you give them up, John, you'll have to give them up absolutely. Sell every dog and never go to a trial again. Not even to judge. John, you couldn't do it."

After a bit, John Angus told how his Cap dog had gripped at the Queen Mother's Trial. One ewe had been crazy, bolting to this side and that, until, Cap lost all patience. John Angus laughed, "Cap gripped at the pen and he wouldn't let go. He clung to her all the way off the course, he was that determined to stop her."

Friday morning. In the program of the International Sheepdog Trials, the duke of Atholl says:

Being in the middle of a hill farming area, trials have always been popular, and I know there are many local farmers and shepherds who are greatly looking forward to seeing the best dogs in Britain and Ireland in action, and I'm sure your Society will find that the audience here is both knowledgeable and appreciative. Certainly we will all do our best to make all competitors and spectators feel at home—no doubt the local refreshments will help to do that!

———

Helen Smeaton finds that condescending. The duke's message is signed, "Atholl," and I find that condescending. John Angus laughs, "The man has a snout on him like a hen salmon."

We are racing along, skilled Helen at the wheel, the wee Irish and me in back. John Angus cries, "Helen stop the car. There! Stop the car!"

A hirsel of ewes was grazing the peat bog on the flank of Ben Lawer. "Look," John said. "That'll be one of Alex MacCuish's ewes. She's cowped."

The ewe had slipped into a deep narrow drain, a hundred yards from the road. She was on her back, her feet fluttering feebly, as John Angus squooged across the peat bog toward her. He no more than righted her than she fell down again. The second time, John Angus leaned into her until she had her balance. A prolapse trembled at her anus like a pink balloon— the pressure of her internal organs had forced a bit of intestine out, but she'd be okay, and so said John Angus as he hopped back over the fence, and once more the Buffalo charged.

Up we go, over barren hills where the roads are closed from December until May.

Early this morning, Ray Edwards phoned, and when he heard of Taff's grip, he said John Angus should go back to the tape (of Taff's whistle commands). When Ray wanted Taff around tight at the drive gate, he'd whistle "WHEET!" or if Taff was to come even quicker, "WHET-WHET!" or if he was to come around but get back at the same time (and thus avoid the danger of a grip), "WHEET-WHEET-WHEEEE."

The hills above Fortingall are beautiful and bleak. When we passed a hill where the Forestry Commission had begun planting rows of trees, John Angus turned to the wee Irish: "In forty years," he said, "the only place you'll see a shepherd is in a museum."

On this, the second day of qualifications, the grandstands were packed and the peeps of their stopwatches more numerous, like crickets.

I speak to Philip Hendry, the ISDS secretary who invites me to lunch with the duke. Hamish MacLean comes off after a nice run with his Lynn bitch and is surrounded by men in wellies and waterproofs asking for pups. Does he have any from his last litter? When will he breed her again? "I get eighty pounds for a pup," Hamish warns, but the buyers wave questions of price aside. "Lynn's next pups are spoken for, I'm afraid."

J. M. Wilson once said the proper thing to do with a dog that's qualified at the National is put it away until the International. This sound advice is universally ignored. When a man has a dog that's almost, almost perfect, it's beyond human restraint to leave the dog alone. Instead, they'll work on that slight imperfection, screwing the dog down tighter and tighter until, under the pressure of the big trial, the dog just falls to pieces.

Many a man came off the course today, abashed at problems he'd caused himself, overtraining his dog.

When J. R. Thomas's Jos makes a mux of it, J. R. bends down and gives Jos a half pat, half cuff. Sheepdogs like honesty; they like to know where they stand.

The back portion of the restaurant tent has been partitioned for the ISDS party, the duke and his guests. I don't know tent etiquette. When do I remove my hat?

The duke is a strongly built, portly man who runs a rural business with a castle, enormous acreage, and a hundred full-time employees. He's slightly ill at ease, though able, at Hendry's suggestion, to produce a welcoming speech to sponsors and honored guests. The Welshman sitting beside the duke will host next year's

International at Glamorgan. Glamorgan, he says, has the finest orangerie in Europe outside Brussels.

The fare is plain: beef, potatoes, carrots, jug wine. Some of the guests (myself, I think) have been invited to fill the quota for "Overseas Guests." Midway through the meal, as the duke and the Welshman discuss deer-management techniques, an elderly Canadian at the end of the table gets to his feet and begins filming with a video camera. He interviews his countryman, a burly mustachioed man in a blue parka, seated across the table from the duke.

"Are you having a good time in Scotland?" the filmmaker inquires.

"Oh yeah, fine." The burly Canadian leans into the center of the table. "I'm having lunch with the duke."

The camera swerves to record the duke who rests his fork.

"And we're having this lunch, which ain't too bad, you know, but I hope we don't have to pay for it; I hope it's free."

The duke snaps, "There is no such thing as a free lunch."

Afterwards, when I asked the duke why the trial was at Blair Atholl, he was vague, saying that, of course, this is sheepdog country, and they came to him in 1982 and again this year, and he said yes. "I'm an amateur, really." "Amateur" was a bigger more languorous word out of his mouth than it looks on the page.

Outside the tent, the duke turned to Ray Ollerenshaw, the ISDS chairman, and muttered, "I loathe that."

What he loathed was a minivan, slathered with Day-Glo posters. "No better bone china in Britain" "Your own dog hand-painted on a plate."

I was struck by the number of concession tents and caravans. By British standards for agricultural events, the International Sheepdog Trial is only midsize. Yet, the Bank of Scotland is here, ready to take a farmer's deposit or cash a check. There's a Subaru dealer, and the Alliance Insurance Company. I ask the insurance agent if they insure dogs as well as livestock and they say yes, yes they do. There's a tent midway, in which Davidson's Veterinary Supplies, Lochan Countrywear, and the Highland Confectionery enjoy a brisk trade. A jeweler sells pendants. Glenfiddich has a caravan. There's a bookstall. In the gift shops, popular items include painted porcelain tableaus—shepherd, Border Collie, two ewes; Border Collie with three lambs—and framed prints of the same subjects.

The woman at the Chum Pet food booth gave me a can of dog food. I'd bring it back for Gael: The familiar taste would be like a Christmas haggis for a Scot far from home.

When John Templeton runs Roy, even the Welshmen stop gossiping. I stood with Kenny Brehmer beside the grandstand waiting for the great dog to make his try. A young shepherd leaned out of the bleachers. "You'll be Donald McCaig, then?"

I guess he knew me from my hat.

"Tom Reid couldn't come. He told me to ask about the wee bitch, Gael."

"Oh," I said.

Even in our mountains, Virginia is much hotter than Scotland, and when I brought Gael home, in early July, the grass was waist high on a man. Gael is less than two feet tall. There are no landmarks in a grass jungle, just a wall of plants with sheep path openings and parks they've grazed down. I would stand beside the barn and send Pip to one side and Gael to the other and within moments all I could see of them was their roostertails through the damp grass. I do not know how Gael learned to navigate, how she found her sheep.

Most handlers who work with imported sheepdogs adopt a Scottish dialect but Gael was now in a country where almost everybody else talked strangely. She stayed close to me, paid no attention to my wife, Anne, ignored Pip once they'd settled territorial claims with brief growls.

Although Border Collies are so keen to work—so *justified* by work—they'll work for anybody, they do best once they've bonded to a man (or woman) and understand the nuances of expression and character. It can be a long courtship: ten months to a year. Gael and I were in love; we were not yet a marriage.

There's no sheepdog trialing in Virginia in July and August, and on the farm we try to complete our sheep chores by 10 A.M., before it gets really hot. Dogs are not particularly efficient hot-weather workers—they only sweat through their tongues and the pads of their feet, and willing Border Collies can literally be worked to death in the heat. If a dog survives heat stroke or convulsions, he'll be susceptible ever after. And many a Scottish dog, imported from a cooler climate, has been ruined on a single scorching hot American afternoon. Although Gael was smooth coated and thus slightly more heat tolerant, her body would take time to adjust.

Gael is a soft dog, quick to learn, calm around stock. When she was weaned from her mother, Tom Reid turned her over to the retarded girl who raises all his pups, gives them the attention and cuddling they require. At eight months, when she showed interest in stock, Tom broke her to work. "She'd slip in with the sheep every chance she had and it was the devil to catch her." Once he had her settled into a fetch and her balance was right, he loaned Gael to a shepherd pal who was lambing. At a year and six months, Gael met hirsels of wild sheep on a great Hill. The work taught her what she needed to know: that if she rushed her sheep, cut in on them, came up short, she had to do the job over and it was always harder the second time. Reid ran Gael at a couple nursery trials, but she was too strongly right-handed. Often pups settle a young bitch, and it worked with Gael. When I met her, at Dalrymple, she'd just run her first open trial.

Although I had a tape of Reid's whistles, I didn't use them at first. We repeated the lessons Gael learned as a puppy. At first, I simply walked her. If, unasked, she went to the sheep and brought them to me, I'd call her off: "That'll do, Gael, here." It was three weeks before I sent her for sheep. WHSSST. From that point, quite slowly, we began reprising her training.

American sheep are, generally, heavier than Scottish sheep, much harder for a dog to move. The dog is trained for working big spaces with sheep who'll bolt when the dog's within a hundred yards. Most of our work is in ten-acre pastures and the dog must haunt her sheep, working within twenty feet of their tails.

Gael is smaller than most Border Collies and her smooth style doesn't upset her sheep. She has no grip in her. This advantage turns to disadvantage with sick or stubborn sheep—she'll bring them, but very slowly. No big problem on the farm but difficult on a trial course with a time limit.

Thus, the wee bitch needed to learn a new language, climate, landscape, and new work rules as well. She finally compromised on a grip. She never did learn to bite a sheep but when a ewe is being particularly hateful she'll jump at her face and snap her teeth and that usually does the job.

With ordinary luck, Gael should continue to improve until she's seven or eight. Older, she'll be wiser, but her body will start to slow down.

I didn't say any of this at the International to Tom Reid's friend. What I said was, "I am well pleased with Gael."

"Aye, Tom will be glad to hear that," the young man said and we both turned to watch Templeton's Roy.

John Templeton and Roy have won the International Driving Championship (Aberystwyth), the International Doubles Championship (Strathaven, Bonchester Bridge, Glasgow, York) and three National championships. Roy has been in the Scottish team every year since 1981. But Roy is 9½ years old. Internationals have been won by dogs Roy's age, but it's uncommon.

As Roy went out, Kenny Brehmer turned to me, "Aye Donald. Have you seen any good dogs here then?"

I replied that, yes, I had. "A few of them are good enough to be competitive in America." Just two Scots pivoted to identify the daft American. Other Scots shuddered like a collective chill had passed through all of them.

John Templeton's commands tumble over one another like a burn over rocks, liquid and quick. Roy steps this way or that. That's when I count the commands: 17 in 15 seconds, and they're so soft, I've missed some.

The Scots forget the brash American to watch a legendary dog. "Look at the bloody wee machine," someone breathes.

John Angus and I leave after Stuart Davidson's run. Helen had left earlier, with the Welshmen. She'd chores to do before she dressed for the International dinner.

At a motorway convenience store, John stops for petrol and a gray-haired woman comes to fill our tank. She remarks that it's been nice weather for a sheepdog trial, and John says, "Aye, but my Taff dog had a grip. He was doing grand until he came to the drive gate, and when I whistled him round, he gripped that horned ewe and cowped her. They want such a tight turn at that panel. Bloody tight turns! Taff's never done a thing like that before."

The woman cuts the pump, "Well, it's been nice weather for it."

As we race back to Kiltyrie, John Angus says that

yesterday the four judges didn't agree whether Taff had gripped or not. "It was two for me and two against." The English judge insisted they call John off.

I say that I met the Welshman who would sponsor next year's International, that it would be at Glamorgan, Wales, that they have the second finest orangerie in Europe.

"Aye," John says, "I'm told that course is a bit dodgy on the left."

When we pulled into the steading at Kiltyrie, Helen came out and looked at both of us, "What have you done with the wee Irish?" she demanded.

Blair Castle sits smack on the main route through the central Highlands. In 1745, Bonnie Prince Charlie stopped here with his Jacobite army on their march south. Later in the rebellion, the castle was occupied by English forces, and Lord George Murray, Charlie's commander, unsuccessfully besieged it. If the castle had fallen to Lord George, perhaps the English army, its flank exposed, might have delayed its march to Culloden, and Charlie might have fought better if he'd fought another day.

I doubt the Jacobite cause might ever have prevailed, but history does like a joke, and we have one here at Blair Castle: a Jacobite redoubt that thwarted a Jacobite assault and tonight celebrates sheepdogs, whose final brilliance was polished on the hard hills created by the Clearances.

For Scotland, Bonnie Prince Charlie's adventure was a political and military disaster. But Jacobite sentiment (half fierce, half embarrassed) lives on in remote rural Scotland, and tomorrow, at the International Sheepdog Trial, many Scots will wear Charlie's emblem—sprigs of white heather—in their lapels.

Blair Castle is a storybook castle, chunky and

white. Queen Victoria granted the dukes the right to maintain the only private army in Britain: the Atholl Highlanders. They are, today, a gentlemen's drill team and social club whose principal function is to supply a piper and fusiliers to fire the courtyard cannon for the tourists.

The sprawling three-story structure is filled with museum-quality antiques and funky stuff. There's a splendid collection of china: Wedgwood, Sevres, Meissen, Derby (complete with photostats of the original bills). A music stand in the drawing room holds the score of the Atholl Quadrilles by one Finlay Dun. Blair Castle is a family home, four hundred years of things people just couldn't bear to throw away. There's a moth-eaten tartan (two hundred years old), intricately cut paper passes worked with the names of executed Jacobites. After Charlie's exile, these would pass you into Jacobite gatherings (and gloomy gatherings they must have been, too). In the same case are cameos of Charlie and the last garter he wore on his deathbed in Rome.

Blair Castle is chockablock with arms and armor, but its bookroom is the size of my linen closet (its linen closet is the size of my house). For a castle, this is a chipper sort of place, willing to be silly. Beside a William-and-Mary state bed, with weary silk hangings and sullen ostrich plumes, a descriptive card worries about the bed's provenance, noting it might not have been in Holyrood (where legend had placed it) and cheerfully concluding, "The search continues!"

The ballroom makes a great postcard, and I bought a dozen of them. It has a hunting-lodge flavor, with stag horns on the creamy end walls and naked wooden trusses supporting the splendid wooden roof.

Arriving a little late—we had the wee Irishman's suit in the car if he tracked us down here—we met Stuart Davidson at the castle's front door. I thought

Stuart had won the qualifying today, but the judge's placed him third, after Adam Waugh and Meirion Jones. Stuart made light of it.

As we passed through the narrow passageway enroute to the bar, John Angus paused to rate each set of antlers. Most, in John Angus's view, were none too good.

We sat at table with Alec Barbour, the duke's factor; Mr. Tull, the farm manager; and Mrs. Tull. The farm manager wasn't feeling well and didn't have much to say. John Angus and the factor fell into a spirited discussion of deer poachers and rogues of their acquaintance. The wine labels read, "Bottled especially for Blair Castle"; the Scotch broth was excellent, the lamb overdone. Helen took a phone call from the wee Irish. He'd found another bed. Would we bring his suitcases to the trial in the morning?

In his after-dinner toast, the duke quoted pastoral poets and lamented that the shepherd's dog has never been as honored as the shepherd. The duke offered his hope "that the shepherd's dog may find his proper place in literature," and the shepherds, not keen readers, most of them, said, "Hear, hear."

Helen was pleased that the speeches were short. The tables were pushed to the walls, and dancing began. Farmers in dress tartan kilts, their wives in gala finery, sailed into St. Bannerman's Waltz and The Pride of Erin. I'm no dancer, so I stepped outside with Alec Barbour. The International was here, he said, from the tradition of Scottish hospitality (the same hospitality that had me—and the wee Irish—at Kiltyrie). "The duke wouldn't say no," he said. "Blair Castle was one of the first of the great houses to open its doors to the public."

We strolled around back of the hulking white ghost, lit with floodlights so motorists could see it from the A9. Alec pointed out the duke's quarters—a homey one-story extension, possibly servant's quarters at one time or stables. The duke of Atholl's living space was less grand than many homes in wealthy American suburbs. Of course, the attached castle had grandeur to spare.

Inside, highlanders danced The Dashing White Sergeant and the Edsome Reel. Women flirted. Men brought trays of drinks from the bar. Helen led me onto the dance floor. She was a splendid dancer and, remembering Pat McGettigan, I avoided stepping on her foot. Men sweated through their white shirts, jokes were told, funny lies. It was one o'clock, soon after they called "Time, gentlemen," when the murmuring started, the music dribbled to a stop, and eyes turned toward the table where we'd had dinner. Strong men surrounded the table, "Give him air." "Is there a doctor? A doctor, please?"

Mr. Tull, the farm manager, lay flat on his back, shirt open, his jacket beside him. Burly men pumped his chest and breathed for him. "He wasn't drinking, no." "They've phoned for an ambulance from Pitlochry."

His damp white shirt stretched across his back, John Angus MacLeod knelt gently at the man's feet. Delicately, like he might touch a failing lamb, he took the man's left hand for a moment, held it, laid it down.

The CPR team was noisy. When they started to thump Mr. Tull's chest, we went out and sat in the bar. Another Scot was talking nervously about a handler who had a great run at the National and after he came off the course, he vomited, knelt beside the water tub, you know, the one they keep to cool the dogs, and took a drink from it and splashed water on his forehead and fell over, then.

Helen looked at John Angus.

John Angus said no, the farm manager was gone. "I took his little finger and bent it back and there was no pulse in there. If you can't get a pulse there . . ."

After the ambulance arrived, we left through the corridor of deer horns. A glass of water in her hands,

Mrs. Tull sat in a straight-back chair, surrounded by friends, inconsolable.

Fifteen dogs ran for the Supreme Championship, Saturday, the final day of the International Sheepdog Trial. The hill on the right hand of the course was a crazy quilt of rust-colored bracken and dark purple heather. The hill was muscular, like a wrestler's shoulder. Feathery stands of Scotch pine and grasses, light and medium green, fringed the base. Count the specks, one, two, three—there are a hundred sheep up there once you get to looking for them, but they're only visible when the light bounces off their wool. That cairn, a spike on the brow of the hill, is a shepherd's cairn, erected to relieve some poor soul's loneliness. The cairn is a beeline three miles from the packed grandstands.

On the left hand, the slope is gentler, and there are horse jumps in the field where cattle graze. Behind the top end of the course, is another, greater hill. Lush fields, outlined by drystane walls, cling to its slopes. They are green as any fields in Wales.

Since yesterday, they've expanded the course. The qualifying trials were run in the lower bulb of a squash-shaped field. For the Supreme Championship, they'll use the upper bulb as well. This is the big course. Ten sheep will be put out half a mile from the handler's stake. The time limit is increased, too; man and dog will have thirty minutes to get the work done. There's a copse of ancient trees between the spot where the first lot of sheep will be put out and where the second lot will appear on the other side of the course.

From where I sit, the sheep look like spilled rice.

The announcer says that a black-and-white bitch has been found roaming loose, and the owner can pick her up at the secretary's tent.

An English shepherd, John Chamberlain, steps onto

the course with his six-year-old tricolor dog, Sam. Although John and Sam barely made the English team, they do a fine job today. When Sam runs out just to the place where he found sheep yesterday, he pauses, and three sharp whistles tell him, "No Sam. They're not there today."

An able dog must be able to accept contradictions. Any rational dog will remember where he found sheep yesterday and will turn in of his own accord to gather them. His handler must correct him just at the point where the dog's faith is already stretched thin. Convinced until this moment that today's is just another routine job of work, the dog is jolted by these new commands and is cast off again, farther, into the wilderness. Sam accepts the correction and sails out, out, hundreds of yards until he finally spots his sheep. Stop: okay; lift: okay; the fetch is a bit zig-zaggy but the sheep go properly through the fetch gate and now, at this moment, the dog is told to abandon his sheep and swing back for a second lot of ten ewes.

The double lift is a special feature of the International Sheepdog Trial's Supreme Championship. On the enormous course here at Blair Atholl, it tests the dog and, not incidently, the dog's man, to the very limit of communion between them.

The dog has already gone out two-thirds of a mile to gather and fetch ten sheep. The moment he gets them back near the man, the man asks him to forget about them, face away; go back for more sheep out there, out of sight, somewhere. Sheepdogs are conservative souls, and this is like asking a New York City widow to lay her social security money on the sidewalk and go into the South Bronx for a bag of gold. "Don't worry. The money'll still be here when you get back."

Faith alone sends the dog back out over the dips and rises until he finds his sheep. Sam finds his. He fetches them back to where he left the first ten, brings all to John Chamberlain's feet, drives them away, crossdrives them—just the same as yesterday.

Five sheep are marked with red ribbons. In the shedding ring, Sam and Jack must shed off fifteen while retaining the ribboned ones. Just so.

The first few sheep come off easily; the dog comes through, splits them off, and they trot away. If the handler is fortunate, these sheep pause to graze close enough so their mates can see them but not so near that the lot in the shedding ring will bolt to join them. They should act as a magnet, but a weak magnet.

The bravest sheep are earliest shed. As man and dog work, the sheep get more worried and soon, only coward sheep remain pressed into the center of the ribboned sheep, determined not to be selected out.

The shedding gets harder as you go.

It takes approximately eighteen minutes for a dog to lift, double lift and fetch the sheep to the man. Man and dog have a dozen minutes remaining for drive, crossdrive, shed and getting the five ribboned sheep into a pen. It's not enough time. Sam takes off seven unribboned sheep. Two more. Then, he works two loose and they run after the nine, but a ribboned sheep decides to go with them, so these three have to be regathered. While Sam is busy doing this, the unshed sheep stroll out of the shedding ring. Sam puts the three, plus the unshed vagrants, back in the ring. Sam sheds a pair, another pair; two unribboned sheep are left now, these very difficult, and time running, time running, got one! The final unribboned sheep is practically impossible, and she's a big one, too, you'd think she'd be willing to chance it. Sam slips in among the ribboned sheep like a snake to sort her off. As she bounces away Sam turns and marches the ribboned five into the pen with seconds to spare.

It was a workmanlike job, not especially stylish. But on a course this size, a shrewd man just tries to get through it within the time limit, and John Chamberlain and Sam will come in second this day.

In his three-piece suit, his fore-and-aft, his dress crook, and leather-covered brass spyglass, John Angus MacLeod is the perfect picture of the shepherd-stalker. For the first time since Taff gripped, John Angus is happy. Earlier, he talked to two Irishmen who'd seen (they said) the whole thing, and this is what they reported: "When yon gimmer came through the gate, she challenged Taff and Taff would have none of it. So he took her by the hind leg and upset her. He cowped her and then, 'Taff put his paw upon her.' Did you hear, Donald? Taff put his paw upon her!"

The mental picture of Taff, rampant, upon a cowped sheep satisfies John Angus. He is done mourning.

The Supreme Championship intimidates men, no less than dogs. Men who run a hundred trials a season pale when they go to this post. Alasdair Mundell is a cool head—there's no cooler head in Argyll. Alasdair was the only Scottish handler to qualify two dogs—Craig and his Meg bitch—at the National, but yesterday he gave Meg Craig's whistle at a critical moment and Meg failed to make the finals. Today, Alasdair and Craig come on the course far too early, before the previous man and dog are off. Then, Alasdair sends Craig out before his sheep are properly on the course, and Craig (who is annoyed) charges a ewe on his lift and repeats the charge on the "Go back" lift, but settles then until he brings his sheep to the shedding ring, where Alasdair is baffled. He can only count four ribboned sheep.

This fluke put the pair in desperate trouble. Alasdair could, and does, ask for time out, for a judge to come onto the field, verify the ribbonless sheep, and designate a replacement, but their working rhythm was shattered, and in trialing, like most sports, everything depends on simplicity and pace.

They got it sorted out, but Craig had had enough,

and when a ewe challenged him, Craig gripped and was disqualified.

At trials in the States, first-time spectators often tell me why the dogs do it. Some attribute it to love. "They must *really* love you!" Others, Skinnerites presumably, prophesy, "I'll bet he'll get a good bone tonight!"

Honestly amazed at the dogs' skills, they are compelled to trivialize them and transmogrify the dogs into lovey-dovey pets, motivated by a dizzy love for their masters, or chowhounds, concerned only with their gut. None of them, not one, has ever *asked* me why the dogs do it. I find the absence of that question only slightly less interesting than the question itself.

Patrick Byrne is a young man and dresses in a casual jacket and slacks, not the suit and tie older shepherds favor. His four-year-old Dot bitch is out of Templeton's Roy and Watson's Mossie. At yesterday's qualifying, the Scottish handlers liked the looks of Dot, more so since it was presumed that a young Irish handler would need an exceptional dog to do as well as Patrick did.

Few knew how sick Dot was. She'd picked up a virus and hadn't eaten for three days. The vet told Patrick, "If she were mine, I wouldn't run her," and Patrick waited beside the reserve member of the Irish team, undecided, until they called his name. "I won't get this chance again," he said.

Today, the young bitch runs out splendidly but has trouble at the fetch. Her sheep don't want to come down the course and keep spreading out on her. Dot takes her "Go back" whistle nicely and makes a second gather, but once again her sheep are slow to move. Perhaps she lacks a bit of power, perhaps she still isn't feeling right.

Since her first lot had decided to drift back up the course hundreds of yards, toward where they'd been let out, Dot's slow progress is excruciating.

When Dot brings her second bunch in, the first is

long gone—split up, one packet near the let-out post, another grazing contentedly farther up the field.

Patrick whistled Dot back for her third outrun, and once she picked up the near packet, he whistled her for the rest, nearly at the far end of the course, almost a mile away. Gallantly, Dot brought the strays together, down the course; joined her second lot; and began her fetch before the judge signaled, "Time!"

Patrick Byrne doffed his cap to the grandstand's applause, patted his brave bitch, and they came off the course together.

There's a well-known American handler (call him "Jake") who imports all his dogs from Britain. Jake's been a trial man for a good many years and is a formidable competitor. Words are not his friends. Whenever I've asked him for an explanation of dog training or trial strategy, his answers are unintelligible.

For many years, whenever Jake brought in a new dog or bitch, the first thing he did was give it a thrashing. To show it, he said, who's boss.

I suppose I must assure you how peculiar this behavior is. Undoubtedly handlers thrash dogs in fits of temper, no doubt a corrective shake is occasionally required during the training of some Border Collies. But there are other dogs who can't be struck at all, and none routinely. In three months in Scotland, I never saw a handler lay a hand on a dog. When Taff gripped—clearly a dog failure, not a man failure—John Angus gave him a pat and put him up and never brought the matter to Taff's attention. John Angus, viewed the grip as a disruption of their communion.

What is interesting about Jake isn't that he beats his dogs, it's how well they work for him. Jake attributes that to the beatings. *Post hoc ergo propter hoc.*

Meirion Jones, a Welshman, and Spot (ROM, registered on merit) laid down a simple, nearly perfect run. Spot's outfield work was flawless and inbye, he lost a few points when three of his twenty sheep bolted around the end of the drive panel. Shedding was handsome, brisk. Meirion Jones rushed matters at the pen and would be penalized slightly for that, but penned successfully.

"This'll be the run to beat," John Angus said.

You can work a bitch in heat beside most sheepdogs and so long as the dog's working, too, the male will ignore her. If you were to dangle a nice juicy kidney before Taff at the handler's post, he'd think you'd gone round the bend.

Unlike most dog breeds, Border Collies are frequently bought and sold when they are middle aged and fully trained. I've known dogs who've had eight different owners. Sometimes a man will sell a dog and several owners later, repurchase it.

Sheepdogs have as various personalities as do men: shy, cocky, aggressive, retiring. Many are excitable; others are calmer. A sheepdog can work for a man and not give a damn for him. Must the actor love the director?

It was getting late. The light was lowering on the trial field, the hilltops and shepherd's cairn were gone in the mist.

Stuart Davidson's Moss had won the Scottish National and yesterday's Brace Championship (with Craig, his running mate) and made a beautiful qualifying run.

Moss picked up his first lot of sheep well enough but went so wide on his "Go Back" that he jumped the course fence and disappeared into the woods, and it was long minutes before he jumped back into the field. Confused, he almost crossed over, but in the nick of time, he spotted his sheep and came around properly behind them. He joined the two groups, started his drive, and everything settled until the drive gate, when all the sheep flinched at some figment of the sheep imagination and trotted around the outside of the gate. Stuart Davidson had come onto the course today to win, and by the time his sheep were in the shedding ring, he was furious. That jump over the fence and missed gate had cost him dearly in points and time. With minutes remaining, Stuart and Moss changed gear. Suddenly, things got funny. With Moss on one side, Stuart on the other, shed sheep just flew off—big batches and little ones. Moss never ran through; he just eyed them until they broke. It was like the Keystone Kops, and the crowd loved it: flying sheep, man and dog on a roll. When a ribboned sheep came off with two unribboned ones, Stuart sent Moss after her. Don't ask me how a dog can select a ribboned sheep from two unribboned ones. I'd never seen it before. We all cheered when that ribboned ewe trotted back into the ring alone.

Stuart was in such a hurry to get to the pen he almost fell over, and his five sheep broke halfway around the pen before Moss stopped them. No more nonsense: They went in. As Stuart slammed the gate, he raised an arm high, like he was directing the cheers for his dog.

In the States, Border Collies often meet their first sheep at sheepdog handlers' clinics, where twenty or so dogs work one at a time, under the supervision of an expert trainer. Many of these dogs are family pets, greatly beloved by their owners. For sheepdogs, they live in the lap of luxury.

Whether eight months old or five years, they walk into the pen with the sheep and goof around and shun the sheep until some movement, some attitude, alerts them and they *see* sheep. It is a brilliant transformation: from being *dog* they become *sheepdog*. They drop down in a crouch, their tails drop below their hocks, their eyes flare, and they start to work the sheep. At this point, usually, the instructor takes over, introducing the dog to his new world. Like as not, the dog's owner is more ignorant than the dog—a fact the dog soon senses. Frequently, a dog who shows great promise when the instructor works him backslides and plays like a puppy when the owner takes command.

I'd hate to see who the dog would go to if the instructor and the owner both called "Here!" at the same time. Sheepdogs don't confuse love with know-how, though frequently their owners do.

Heflin Jones, a Welshman, with 5-year-old Meg, was last to run. Although they didn't complete their shed, the pair had enough points to come in third today. Despite his last-minute acrobatics, Stuart Davidson came in fourth.

As the crowd pours out of the grandstand, the International Sheepdog Society gathers in the infield to award its grandest trophy: the heavy International shield, a plaque ringed with the names of eminent dogs.

The duke's black Labrador retriever lies with his posterior toward the crowd, does not acknowledge the Border Collies, and never takes his doting eyes off the duke.

Meirion Jones is awarded the International shield, the Chum Supreme Championship trophy, the Sun Alliance silver tray, and the Caithness Glass award. Patrick Byrne and Dot get the sportsmanship award. As the International Team gathers for the official photograph, the duke bends to pat Meirion Jones's Spot, and Spot jumps to the end of his lead, alarmed and amazed.

The media here today are the *Scottish Farmer* and *Working Sheepdog News* and yours truly. Photographers' flashes brighten the twilight. The second time the duke bends to pet Spot, Spot lets him do it.

For four hundred years, sheepdogs have been bred for a complex set of skills and desires. Inept dogs were put down. Thus, genetically, most sheepdogs have a rough idea what to do. The trainer refines that idea and explores, with the dog, some of life's contradictions.

The dog must be instantly biddable but be able to think for himself.

The dog must be able to bring a stroppy tup to his knees but never nip a lamb, even when the lamb runs right over him.

A good working collie uses reason to support his faith.

The trial dog needs great courage (how would you like to do the most difficult bits of your daily work before two thousand knowledgeable spectators?); a temperament that can handle stress, and, finally, style. When an eminent dog joins a dangerous man, they can create a performance that is, by either standard—dog's or man's—beautiful.

That's why the dogs do it: because it's beautiful. When a sheepdog meets a man able to help him create beauty, the dog will put up with almost anything. It's sad when eminent dogs are given shoddy goods, "sumbitches" to work with.

As the handlers load their dogs and trophies, John Angus spots Eric Halsell, the BBC sheepdog commentator and pursues him through the parking lot crying, "Points off, eh Eric! Points off!" The little man blanches and gets away from this lunatic highlander as quickly as he can.

Back home, it'll be cooler and our trial season just beginning. This fall, I'll run Gael, and Pip, so long as he is able. The best single day Pip and I ever had on the trial field, we came fifth, and years later I can remember details of his run. In other hands, Pip might have become eminent; he *was* good enough to teach an ignorant man how to work a sheepdog. Gael, and every other new, young dog I'll train will owe him that debt. Pip, a forty-five pound, black-and-white dog, changed my life.

Departing cars at Blair Atholl have made a morass at the gate, and I'm grateful that Helen is at the wheel. As we wait for the cars ahead to get through the deep muddy spots, Helen says that next year, for the International, they might rent a caravan.

John Angus is still laughing, "Did you hear me with that wee man? 'Points off! Points off!' "

"With a caravan we could make breakfast and have a cup of tea whenever we wanted."

"Yes," John Angus says, "and it'd be easier on the dogs. Are we going to Wales, then?"

"Aye."

"You're very confident. How do you know I'll make the Scottish team?"

"Well, John, you'd just better pull your socks up and get to it." And Helen gunned the car through the mud and away.

If this has persuaded you to buy a Border Collie for a pet, I have done you and your dog a disservice. If you don't have work for a Border Collie, or time to train it properly, your bright young Border Collie will invent his own work, and chances are you won't like it.

There are dozens of dog breeds bred to be good pets. If a pet is what you seek, you should choose among them.

ACKNOWLEDGMENTS

I'd like to thank those shepherds, farmers, sheep-dog admirers, and book people whose hospitality and generosity of spirit made this book possible.

In Britain

Mr. and Mrs. John Bathgate
Geoff and Viv Billingham
Mr. Kenny Brehmer
Mrs. E. B. Carpenter
Mrs. Ian (Marjory) Chapman
Mr. and Mrs. Stuart Davidson
Mr. and Mrs. Peter Hetherington
Mr. A. Philip Hendry, Esq.
Mr. Douglas Lamb
Mr. and Mrs. J. P. Mackenzie
Mr. and Mrs. Hamish MacLean
Mr. J. A. MacLeod
Mr. Alasdair MacRae
Mr. and Mrs. David McTeir
Mr. and Mrs. Alasdair Mundell
Mr. Boyd Mundell
Mr. Matt Mundell
Mr. and Mrs. Bill Merchant
Mr. Tom Reid
Ms. Helen Smeaton
Mr. and Mrs. Jock Richardson
Mr. David Sutherland
Mr. John Templeton, M.B.E., and Mrs. John Templeton

In the States

Ms. Kathy Banks
Mr. Knox Burger
Mr. Edward Burlingame
Mrs. Bryan Conrad
Ms. Vicki Hearne

And thanks to Pip and Gael—without whom the story would have been completely different.